Return

Past Life Regression and You

D1490817

Return

Past Life Regression and You

by

Dr. Georgina Cannon

Toronto, Canada

Ontario Hypnosis Centre
Suite 310, 94 Cumberland Street
Toronto, Ontario M5R 1A3
Phone: (416) 489-0333 Toll Free: (866) 497-7469 Fax: (416) 484-8546
email: info@returntopastlife.com
www.returntopastlife.com

National Library of Canada Cataloguing in Publication

Cannon, Georgina

Return : past life regression and you / by Georgina Cannon.

Includes bibliographical references and index.

ISBN 0-9735311-0-X

1. Reincarnation therapy. 2. Hypnotism—Therapeutic use.

I. Title.

RC489.R43C35 2004   616.89'14   C2004-902628-3

Editor: Penny Hozy
Book design : Karen Petherick,
Intuitive Design International Ltd.

Printed in Canada

This book contains information from highly respected sources –
all of which are named and cited in the Notes. However the author cannot assume responsibility for the validity of all materials or the consequences of their use.

Caveat

The author advises the reader that when self-facilitating into self-hypnosis, it is essential to be fully sober, conscious and alert, in the present and grounded when going into and coming out of self-hypnosis, otherwise you may feel disoriented for a short while, as if suddenly waking up from a deep sleep. It is recommended that you re-enter your present life with caution, gently and slowly. The reader (and not the author) assumes full responsibility for his or her own journey through this and other lifetimes, for all the consequences of any and all mental or physical activity undertaken as a result of reading this book, or in attempting to apply, in any way, anything discussed or described therein.

This book is not intended to replace the need and requirement for medical or other applicable therapeutic assistance. The author does not claim that anything written in this book is the solution, in part or in whole, to any mental, physical or spiritual problem and must not be relied on as such. The author urges the reader to obtain assistance and advice from an appropriately qualified person prior to attempting to apply, in any way, anything discussed or described in this book.

Table of Contents

Acknowledgements

First I must acknowledge the guidance of Henry Bolduc, who not only introduced me to the power of facilitating Past Life Regression, but also demonstrated how to teach it by putting aside the self. This lesson has served me well in the clinic and school.

Next, I want to thank all the clients and students over the years from whom I have received both wisdom and humility in sharing their extraordinary soul journeys.

To my clinic colleagues and staff, who work brilliantly with our clients, facilitating daily miracles, who challenge, guide and support me, I couldn't have written this without your commitment to excellence. My longtime colleague and friend, Cathie, always leading and always "getting it" to make the process easier and smoother. And Debbie Lockie who keeps my feet on the ground while I soar.

To the daughter of my heart, Cassandra, my birth family in Israel and Toronto, and my family of choice, my friends in Toronto, New York, Spain, England and Hong Kong, you are my gift and I am always grateful and thrilled with the reservoir of joy, giggles and unconditional love available to me.

To CBC producer Sarah Kapoor, who had the curiosity and interest to spread the word through television, and integrity in choosing the perfect team and crew, who worked together with respect for the process and kindness for the volunteers and me.

Finally, to Penny Hozy, editor, friend and facilitator. Without her this book would never have made it to print.

… and then there's Charlie … who keeps me laughing. What more could any person want in this lifetime? I am blessed. And I wish the same for you.

Introduction

Why this book – now?

For too long the healing of bodies and the healing of minds have been considered as separate disciplines. The emergence of past life therapy, however, indicates that the holistic approach will again be granted the (respected) status it once enjoyed.

– Joel L. Whitton, MD, PhD, *Life Between Life*

IN THE SUMMER OF 2003, I was approached by a producer from the CBC, Canada's national broadcaster, to participate in a 20-minute segment for a Sunday morning newsmagazine program. After discussing the process of past life regression with her, I suggested that she might be interested in undergoing a past life session herself, and she agreed. From just that one session, she realized the power of past life regression, and took the idea back to the CBC for further discussion and development. The original idea for a 20-minute segment expanded into the idea for three one-hour specials. The reason I said yes to the CBC, after saying no to three other groups who had approached me, was because of their credibility as an organization, but also because they were willing to do the research around the past lives experienced by the people who participated in the program.

During filming, I facilitated past life regression journeys for more than 30 volunteers, most of whom I had never met before or had never been hypnotized before, and many of whom were cynical about the process. Ninety per cent of them went into past lives with a camera inches from their face, bright lights, the movements of the camera crew all around them, and the sounds of an active hypnotherapy clinic happening nearby. Most of the volunteers experienced specific past lives for which they were able to provide significant details. These details, including drawings in some cases, were then handed over to a research team of sociologists, archaeologists, and historians, who were able to verify and document actual lives lived in the past.

For me, it was an intense and exhilarating process that confirmed the need for this book. The show itself helps bring awareness of past life regression in a very practical way to the general public. This book extends that knowledge and awareness because the more people who know the power and potential for healing from past life experiences, the more past life regression will be used, ethically and appropriately, for this purpose.

I'm not trying to convince you of anything. I'm simply presenting ideas, research and work as it has flowed into my life and the lives of my colleagues. So do your own research and decide for yourself whether or not past life regression can help you, or those you love, in this lifetime.

Read this book with a "believe it or not" attitude. See if it's useful for your own journey at this time on this planet. Ultimately this current life is the most important life. Do whatever you need to do to live it fully and with joy.

CHAPTER 1

What *Is* Past Life Regression?

Life is like a string of pearls, the self being the thread, and the pearls side by side are life experiences, births and deaths being a continuum, all opportunities for growth in consciousness. – Barbara Findeisen

LET'S PRETEND FOR A MOMENT that you are sitting peacefully in a comfortable chair and day-dreaming about nothing in particular. Suddenly you get a sense of being somewhere else ... just for a moment. Somewhere that you can see, smell, hear, and also feel emotion.

That's what a past life journey feels and looks like, except it's usually longer – sometimes lasting up to two hours or more – or occasionally shorter, depending on the lifetime experienced.

Remember the last time you were at the movies and you became so involved in the story that you cried? You were emotionally, even physically, involved, but you also knew that there were people around you eating popcorn or whispering comments. That too is what a past life regression journey can feel like. You are *there*, and *here*, at the same time. Sounds strange? A bit perplexing?

Maybe it is. But the feelings and the wisdom coming from the journey are profound and can be life-changing.

I came to hypnosis and past life regression from a life in the corporate world where we used words such as "outcomes" and "deliverables" – a very pragmatic business background. Before that, I was a journalist where I quickly developed a cynicism about anything that appeared to lack credibility. And yet, with all of that, I knew that reincarnation existed and other lives in other times and places were not an anomaly. So when I decided to make past life regression my life's work, through hypnosis and healing, I was determined that it be done in the most professional, ethical, and practical way possible.

I left the corporate world because I was tired of the non-stop politics, game playing and the inability to see people as anything other than human capital. It seemed to me there was more to life than the bottom line. I especially wanted to explore those other parts of myself that contained the heritage of my ancestors.

I studied with Henry Bolduc, whose view of the world and of this work is forthright and honorable. Henry believes that we can regress in order to more wisely move forward.

> Regression work is the process not the product. How you learn and how you use that learning is far more important than who you were and how you lived. The soul's memory is your true wisdom.
> – Henry Bolduc, *Life Patterns*

Dr. Winafred B. Lucas, a psychologist and expert in the field of past life regression, says that physical or emotional pain and disharmony draw our attention to non-aligned aspects of our psyche until we are eventually forced to "right ourselves" and create a homeostatic balance.

On a spiritual level, any journey we take through our past lifetimes is a movement toward karmic homeostasis. As we discover repeated patterns in our past lives, we begin to work through them until we achieve "wholeness" and find a place of balance and harmony.

The life we live today, in the present, on this planet, gives us the opportunity to rectify past mistakes and complete unfinished business, to learn lessons we didn't learn in previous lives in order to perfect ourselves on the soul journey. This process is necessary because the soul needs a spectrum of experiences in order to become complete.

Since I began working with past life regression I have found that sometimes the answers can be discovered in a single past life, at other times the lesson may be repeated over different lifetimes, not always sequentially – and they all have to be cleared, healed and forgiven.

And as to you life, I reckon you are the leavings of many deaths; No doubt I have died myself ten thousand times before.
– Walt Whitman

Return

It's over – again – for a while
Time to revisit
whatever's been and been seen.
You return once more
To peace, a timeless place
in a placeless time.
Soul space,
of quietude and wonder,
of wisdom and learning
Until next time.
The trepidation of a new beginning
the anticipation of a new threshold
the joy of feeling without thought
discovering the world again.
Colour, depth and harmonies,
feet on the earth,
heart in your hands
Exploring
the pure happiness of time
to be, to create, to watch
to do or do nothing;
running or standing still.
Time for you
and a new sunrise on your soul.

Welcome to Your Past, Present and Future!

So I say to you, as you begin your spiritual journey of the soul, welcome to the world of your past, present and future! Welcome to the opportunity to regress and discover memories you only thought you had forgotten. You are embarking on a journey that could change your life by bringing the wisdom and understanding of other lifetimes into your current life.

You've heard the expression, "Things are more than they appear to be." In the case of soul journeys, that's definitely true. If we start from the premise that we're all energy and everything around us is all energy – just a different frequency – we can understand that energy never stops, it just recycles into something else. For instance, light is energy, color is energy, even the chair you're sitting on now is an energy frequency that gives the appearance of solidity so that you can sit on it safely. If you have trouble wrapping your head around that, how about the concept that energy is never wasted? A flower blooms and dies, a seed falls to the ground and is nourished by previous death to bloom again. And so it is with animals and all of nature.

Physicists confirm that energy fields, which include behavior patterns – the body itself is an energy field – cannot simply cease to be, they can only be transmuted. Albert Einstein talked about consciousness – consciousness as energy – as a fundamental aspect of existence. Shamans, healers and other mystics from the past under-stood the power of using the altered state to retrieve memories while the conscious mind processed them to bring understanding.

It's like deja vu all over again.
– Yogi Berra

I am confident that there truly is such a thing as living again, that the living spring from the dead, and that the souls of the dead are in existence.
– Socrates

Exploring your own birth and death cycles, which we call reincarnation, is a joyful, inspiring and humbling experience. If you're ready to go on that journey, come and join me.

People like us, who believe in physics, know that the distinction between past, present, and future is only a stubbornly persistent illusion.

– Albert Einstein

What To Know Before You Go: A Code of Ethics

Before we begin, there is one very important point that needs to be made. Whether you decide to experience past life regression yourself through this book and disk, or whether you choose a facilitator to lead you there, there is a code of ethics that needs to be honored and adhered to. It is my goal that soon, all well-trained facilitators will display a code of ethics in their clinics. (See Addenda for the complete Code of Ethical Conduct.)

**Make sure the environment you choose
for the journey feels safe and you can trust your
facilitator.**
You'll be entering the altered state of hypnosis and although you'll be in complete control through your conscious mind, if you feel safe and relaxed you'll be more inclined to let the memories come to the surface easily and effortlessly.

**Request your soul's permission
before embarking on the journey.**
Permission is obtained by going deep inside yourself to that quiet space within and asking if it is "appropriate that I journey to another time and another place at this time." And listen with your heart for the answer. There will always be a definite yes or no.

**Protection and help must be asked for
before you embark on the journey.**
Whether you embark on this journey alone or with a facilitator, see, feel and sense a protective white light around you to keep you safe from any unwelcome energies. If you are in touch with your spiritual guides or angels, this is the time to ask for them to journey with you.

Before the closing curtain drops on a past lifetime, send compassion and forgiveness and love to yourself as you were in that life.
Each life is a process of learning and many times the past life memory is not something we would choose to explore. It may well be that we once lived a life of which, today, we are not proud. But that was then, and this is now. So forgive and let it go.

Before the closing curtain drops on that lifetime, send forgiveness, compassion and love to those who shared that life with you.
Remember that people choose their actions and behaviors. Some behavior is neither pleasurable nor beneficial to us, but it enriches our knowledge of who we are and how we are. They too are living the journey they need, so bring understanding and forgiveness into that time, recognizing the role of learning for both of you. (Forgiveness is letting go of pain – so why not do it?)

Explore and bring forward the joy and wisdom from that life into the present time.
This will allow you to benefit from the experience and absorb the joy and wisdom to enhance your current life.

Close off the life, let the curtain or veil drop, leaving all pain and discomfort behind the veil, in that lifetime where it belongs.
This allows you to use the knowledge gained in the current life journey, which may or may not include pain of its own.

Return in fullness to the current time and place, fully encouraged and with permission to bring your experience into your current lifetime.
Once that file has been opened, new understandings will emerge from time to time. This will allow you to remain open to the learning and wisdom you have acquired.

CHAPTER 2

Memory Versus Imagination

Memory is history recorded in our brain, memory is a painter, it paints pictures of the past and of the day. – Grandma Moses, artist

A Bit About Hypnosis

HYPNOSIS WAS ORIGINALLY DEFINED as "an increase in suggestibility." It is the avenue that leads us into the subconscious mind, where our memories are stored, and is a means by which we activate the subconscious mind.

Our conscious mind manages our rational brain activity and harbors our free will, yet it controls only about 10% of our body and brain activity – the active, aware part. Our unconscious mind, on the other hand, is our "memory bank" and houses our perceptions and sensations, as well as our image of our self. The unconscious controls about 90% of our brain and body functions, including our autonomic nervous system. Hypnosis helps us access these functions for both therapeutic and non-therapeutic reasons and is commonly used to explore past lives.

People's brain waves change when they are in a past life regression, and they are different from the brain waves of any other mental state we know of (normal wakefulness, sleep, dreaming, hypnosis alone). – Winafred Lucas, Ph.D.

People often think that being hypnotized means going to sleep (we've all heard of the stage hypnotist who tells the volunteer, "You're getting sleepy, very sleepy") but hypnosis, or trance, has nothing to do with sleep. A number of experimental studies in the 1930's, involving brain waves and other physiological reactions, clearly showed that sleep and hypnosis were different states. Further studies have shown that people experiencing past life regression have unique brain wave patterns.

A Bit About Time

The only reason for time is so that everything doesn't happen at once.
– Albert Einstein

Past life regression is a journey, usually under hypnosis or an altered state, which leads to another time and another place that your soul has experienced in the past. The memory of this experience exists in your subconscious mind. However, time is a human concept. It could be that all our previous lives are lived simultaneous to, or concurrent with, the present life, as if we were looking at the many sides of a prism. Each reflects differently, but the light and the life come from one source.

I Made It Up ... Right?

To believe in the things you can see and touch is no belief at all; but to believe in the unseen is a triumph and a blessing.
– Abraham Lincoln

Many people find that when they come out of their first journey into the past, they can't quite believe that it's true, and they wonder if they made it up.

I usually ask them, made it up out of what? If they had made it up, surely they would have given themselves the life of a king or an empress or a famous film star! Yet, in all the years I have been doing past life regression, and all the discussions I have had with various colleagues, no one has yet met up with a researchable, quantifiable past-life Nero, Cleopatra or Queen Elizabeth I.

Edgar Cayce believed that imagination is the avenue to the visual faculty of the mind. Henry Bolduc's research suggests that hypnosis enhances the image-making part of the mind. He found that people who can consciously visualize seem to do better in hypnosis. In *The Journey Within* he says, "The imagination is not in conflict or opposed to past-life memory. It is a helpful tool."

Here's what else Henry Bolduc has to say on the subject:

> "A common concern is the doubt that some people express regarding the reality of the past-life experience. They wonder if they are making up a story from creative imagination. [I] respond by assuring them that the story received is relevant and valuable to them. If they try to analyze a memory while it is unfolding, they are likely to stop the flow of memory. Technically, that problem occurs because analysis is a left-brain function; memory and recall are associated with right-brain functioning.
>
> "Often, when a past-life regression session is a new experience in the person's current consciousness, it, at first, actually does seem as if it might be imagination. In a matter of minutes, as the person stays with it, the story begins to flow with ease. The memory begins to open in depth, wonder, and sometimes, in amazement."

Carl Rogers, a respected psychologist, admits to having changed his mind about past lives when his friends related their experiences to him.

In the process, he seems to have taken a quantum leap into the future and opened his mind to the infinite possibilities of the human spirit:

> *Perhaps we are entering a transitional stage of evolution similar to that of the first sea creatures who laboriously dragged themselves out of the swampy bogs to begin the difficult and complex task of coping with the problems of living on land ... Are we entering new worlds of psychic space, as well as the world of outer space? What is the future of the human spirit? To me these are tantalizing, but definitely hopeful questions.* – Carl Rogers in *Reincarnation*

So ... Can I Prove It?

One question that's often asked is, can it be proven? And the answer is, yes, in many cases it can, if you wish to take the time and if you have enough factual information, such as names, addresses and dates.

Verification, however, can be a tricky business. While it's one thing to ask a person experiencing a past life what day it is, it's quite another to verify the authenticity of that particular date. Calendars throughout history have measured time using many different systems. The Babylonians used the cycles of the moon. The Egyptians, however, used a solar-based calendar. The lunar cycle is actually 29.53059 days long, and the earth's orbit around the sun is 365.242196 days. The earliest lunar/ solar based Roman calendars showed increasing discrepancies over time. The Julian calendar calculated the solar year at 365.25 days and required an extra day be added every four years to correct the discrepancy. Then there's the Gregorian calendar, which was adopted to correct the creeping time problem created because the Julian year was eleven minutes and four seconds longer than the solar year and slowly but surely drifted out of synch with the seasons. (Do I need to say more?)

Henry Bolduc says that "past lives do not necessarily need to be literal to be helpful."

I encourage people with whom I work not to be distracted by attempts at verification, but to continue on the path of honest, open-minded exploration. Each of us tells a story with our lives - one different from all other stories - our own unique history. Results do not even

When the details and demographic information people report in past life regressions are checked they are almost always accurate.
– Helen Wambach, Ph.D.

The real voyage of discovery is not in seeking new lands but in seeing with new eyes.
– Marcel Proust

require belief. Open-minded inquiry is all that is necessary. – The Journey Within

As I worked with each one of the volunteers for the television show, time and time again they demonstrated to themselves and the filming crew, that the journey itself isn't all there is. It is the learning, the wisdom, the understanding it brings to the current life which makes the trip so profoundly moving.

Apples - Oranges
Red Bell Pepper
Mozzarella Sticks
Splenda

What's In It For Me?

One of the key benefits of doing past life regression is that we gain a deep wisdom that goes beyond our current experience. Quite often people react to a past life experience or memory by asking, "Where did that come from?" The classic Buddhist text, the Dhammapada, says, "All that we are is the result of what we have thought."

Another benefit of past life regression is that we can experience life with a different color skin or a different gender, age, culture, different economic or educational experience, so we get to experience our world from a very different perspective. We begin to realize at a deep level that not everyone has or had readily available food, medicine, order, justice and love.

Past life regression can be a self-healing process. If we heal the past, we can heal the present and the future. By accessing the past and uncovering the patterns of behavior in our lives, we can break the cycle of pain, physical and psychological, that may be plaguing us. By understanding the source of our distress, we can let it go. Past life regression allows us to move beyond whatever is blocking us or holding us back from achieving peace and happiness in our current life. We can expand our awareness and alleviate physical and psychological symptoms – and here's the best part – without drugs or medication!

To attain to the human form must always be a source of joy. And then to undergo continuous transitions, with only the infinite to look forward to: what incomparable bliss is that!
– Lao Tse,
Tao Te Ch'ing

CHAPTER 3

The History of Your History

In the beginning, the universe was created. This made a lot of people very angry, and has been widely regarded as a bad idea.
– Douglas Adams, *Hitchhiker's Guide to the Galaxy*

In the Beginning ... There Was Edgar Cayce

WE CAN'T TALK ABOUT the history of past life regression without acknowledging the work of Edgar Cayce and a few other notable pioneers. There is no way I can include everyone who has made an impact on the profession generally, but here are a few chosen names who have impacted my learning and teaching – to the benefit, I hope, of clients and students!

Edgar Cayce, often called America's "sleeping prophet," was born in Hopkinsville, Kentucky, in 1877. He has been credited with the beginnings of the current holistic health movement. Cayce laid the groundwork for the growing awareness that the mind is a very powerful tool in creating health and wellness.

Cayce recognized in his work that what one thinks and feels emotionally will find expression in the physical body, so that mental patterns can have a direct impact on the physical response whether it is physical good health or disease. Through his personal experience and his readings, Cayce saw that total health requires consideration of the individual's entire being – the physical, mental and spiritual components of life, not just the specific illness.

Up until 1923 there were two sides to Cayce. There was the Cayce who went to church, read the Bible and taught Sunday school. Then there was the Cayce who had visions, heard voices, and could perform medical readings in a self-induced trance. Today we call it self-hypnosis.

But this changed in 1923 when Arthur Lammers asked Cayce to do a reading for him. For 22 years Cayce's readings had been almost exclusively devoted to medical or health issues, but Lammers questioned the sleeping Cayce about matters such as mysticism and reincarnation. When the reading was over, Cayce was astonished that what he said during the trance was foreign to everything he had been taught and believed. Cayce was deeply concerned, especially with the idea of reincarnation, but because he believed so strongly in the truth of his health readings, he reasoned that the new information he had received from what he called a "life reading" must also be true. Reincarnation became central to Cayce's belief system and led to his acceptance of reincarnation and the existence of a "universal consciousness."

From the wisdom gained in those readings Cayce believed that truth is a growing thing and that the element which holds together the huge diversity of being human, is a common spiritual heritage.

For each entity in the earth is what is it because of what it has been! And each moment is dependent upon another moment. So a sojourn in the earth, as indicated, is a lesson in the school of life and experience.
– Edgar Cayce, Readings, 2823-3

HENRY BOLDUC

In the late 1950s, while he was still a teenager, Henry Bolduc read a book that changed his life. That book was *The Search for Bridey Murphy*, the story of a young woman who in hypnosis experienced another lifetime in Cork, Ireland. Henry accepted the book's truth, knowing that it "felt right, touched some hidden core in my being." From that point on he pursued the adventure of duplicating the experiment that had led to the story of Bridey Murphy. Henry Bolduc is a certified hypnotherapist who has spent more than 42 years doing past life research. He has written books, taught seminars and offers his research and wisdom freely to those who are interested in learning about past life regression therapy and healing.

I study how the past fits into my present and where my present is reflected in my past. I then look for ways to build a better future.
— Henry Bolduc

CAROL BOWMAN

Carol Bowman is a leading expert in the field of children's past lives. She became interested in children's past life memories when her own children were young and had memories of other lifetimes. When her son Chase was 5 years old he became extremely frightened of loud noises. With the help of a friend who was a hypnotherapist, Chase described a past life in which he was a soldier who had been wounded in the wrist. When Chase's eczema on his wrist disappeared along with his phobia, Bowman thought there might be a connection. She began to research the phenomenon and eventually developed techniques for parents to use with their children to help them process past-life memories. Bowman continues to promote research into children's past life memories through lecturing and writing books.

 For now we know that children are more than just biological beings shaped by heredity and environment. They are spiritual beings, too, who bring with them wisdom and experience gathered from other lives on earth.

– Carol Bowman, *Children's Past Lives*

WINAFRED BLAKE LUCAS

Winafred Lucas has had a lifetime of academic and professional training in clinical psychology, beginning in the 1930s, with Jungian analysis and forty-five years of clinical therapy with children and adolescents. Her work with regression therapy includes the areas of pre-natal experience and the interlife. Her regression therapy focuses on the belief that physical traumas from past lives can become embedded at an organic level and affect the physical body in the current life. Lucas believes that the life we live today gives us the opportunity to rectify past mistakes and complete unfinished business (i.e., learn lessons we didn't learn, to perfect ourselves).

 The soul needs a spectrum of experiences to become complete. – Winafred B. Lucas

DR. IAN STEVENSON

Ian Stevenson, MD, Professor and Chairman Emeritus of the Department of Psychiatry at the University of Virginia, is a leader in the field of past life recollections in children. He has collected and documented over 2,000 cases of children with experiences of reincarnation. In his research, Dr. Stevenson has found that many of these children carry birthmarks or deformities suffered in a previous life. He has done major scientific work in the study of birthmarks and birth defects among children who remember living before, some from the time before they began to speak. In many of these cases, Dr. Stevenson has documents and photographs confirming injuries suffered in previous lives which leave a mark on the skin we call a birthmark.

 Science should pay a lot more attention to the evidence we have pointing towards life after death. Looked at fairly, the evidence is impressive and from a variety of sources.
– Dr. Ian Stevenson

DR. BRIAN WEISS

Dr. Brian Weiss completed his medical training at the Yale University School of Medicine and is the former chairman of the Department of Psychiatry at Mount Sinai Medical Center in Miami. Trained as a traditional psychiatrist and psychotherapist, Dr. Weiss began to explore past life regression as a means of therapy after one of his patients began recalling past-life traumas that seemed to be connected to her recurring nightmares and anxiety attacks. He was skeptical at first, but when she began to channel messages from "the space between lives," containing revelations about Dr. Weiss's family, he experienced what he calls an epiphany, an awakening to the realization that exploring past lives was a way to cure present-day illnesses. At that point he embarked on a new phase of his career that came to include writing books, presenting national and international seminars and experiential workshops as well as training programs for professionals.

 Although past life therapy can heal significant physical and emotional problems quickly and deeply, it is not necessary to have a serious problem to benefit from this process. Many productive, highly functioning people suffering from seemingly minor problems and worries can also profit. – Dr. Brian Weiss, Through Time Into Healing

ROGER J. WOOLGER, PH.D.

Roger J. Woolger is a Jungian analyst, past life therapist, teacher, lecturer and author of the book *Other Lives, Other Selves.* Dr. Woolger regularly uses past life regression as a modality for healing as part of his psychotherapy practice. His technique expands the Jungian injunction to "stay with the image" by adding a metaphysical and metapsychological framework which allows more than one reality for his patient. He maintains that "the subject must fully re-experience the bodily sensations of the past life for emotional and energetic release to be complete." Otherwise, he maintains, the psychological complex seeking to express itself will remain lodged in the body. Dr. Woolger believes that being aware of one's previous life is a further extension of the Jungian precept to "stay with the image" – only now it is expressed by staying in the image of the other lifetime.

 My [past life] story ... [was] of a very crude peasant-turned-mercenary soldier ... in the papal army raised by the King of France to exterminate heresy ... The most painful recognition of how that soldier still lived in me was remembering one fight I had gotten into at school around 12 years of age. I had become so wild with rage at a boy ... that four other boys had to drag me off him. I had been ready to kill: I vowed never to lose my temper again; a part of me recognized how easily I could kill. [It was] a painful past life memory.

– Roger Woolger PhD, *Other Lives, Other Selves*

I have learned much from studying the lives and writings of these individuals, and others, and have called upon their wisdom many times. They have contributed immeasurably to the advancement of hypnotherapy and past life regression. Their words and ideas are found throughout this book.

The Karma Connection

What some people refer to as Karma, is known to be the sum of all incarnations that form our learning history, and stamps our conduct and emotions. I believe we are born with our Karma, which is like being dealt a hand of cards. How we play those cards is up to us. Do you choose to play poker, solitaire or bridge with your life?

The Hindu concept of the universe comes from understanding that the creative, destructive and neutralizing forces in the universe evolve the principles of *akasha*, *prana* and creative mind. *Akasha* is the substance in all matter, *prana* is the force that moves through matter, and the creative mind is that from which the universe was created.

All these principles are contained in the human body, which has seven levels of consciousness or energy called *chakras*. These lie parallel and close to the spinal column.

The Hindu universal law of action and reaction is called Karma. It is our inheritance brought forth from former lifetimes that shapes our fate and destiny. Tendencies to act according to certain patterns established by reactions from the past are known as *samskaras*. *Vansanas* are memory traces that form this pattern.

For Hindus, Karma decrees complete personal responsibility. While many of us prefer to place the responsibility for our problems outside of ourselves, karmic doctrine claims that every action, every decision has consequences that are determined by the act itself.

You have to learn to fight adversity and to solve (problems). If you do not solve them in this lifetime, they appear again and again in different forms and situations in the same life, and in other ones, until you learn to master them in the right way.
– Dr. Varvara Ivanova, Russian psychiatrist

The Hindus are very aware that experiences from past lifetimes create a large part of our psychological makeup. With this concept comes *atman* or individual soul, and *brahman*, cosmic soul. There is a reservoir of stored-up energy at the base of the spine called *kundalini* with the symbolic representation of a sleeping serpent. In order to reach the highest level of consciousness, the individual soul must unite with the cosmic soul by unleashing this reservoir of energy at the base of the spine and sending it upward to the top of the brain. This can be accomplished through regular deep meditation or yoga. This energy eventually reaches the superconscious state called *samadi*, the ultimate freedom from the cycle of birth and death as well as liberation from all miseries and bondage.

Gandhi once wrote in a letter to his close disciple Madeleine Slade, daughter of British Admiral Sir Edward Slade: "What you say about rebirth is sound. It is nature's kindness that we do not remember past births. Where is the good, either of knowing in detail the numberless births we have gone through? Life would be a burden if we carried such a tremendous load of memories. A wise man deliberately forgets many things, even as a lawyer forgets the cases and the details as soon as they are disposed of. Yes, 'Death is but a sleep and a forgetting.'"

But some of us realize this ending marks a fresh, adventurous beginning after a spiritually creative and healing rest.

Buddhism

Buddhism originated in northern India over 2500 years ago. From there it spread into China, Japan and Tibet. By following Buddhism's Eightfold Path of right understanding, right thought, right speech, right action, right livelihood, right effort, right mindfulness and right concentration, it is possible for everyone to reach Nirvana, a state of bliss that frees the individual from the cycle of birth, death and rebirth.

If you want to know the past, look at your present. If you want to know the future, look at your present.
– Gautama Buddha

As it spread to other parts of the world Buddhism absorbed aspects from the philosophy of its host culture. For example, Zen Buddhism, as practiced in Japan, emphasizes meditation and the experience of sudden insight as the way to reach Nirvana. Zen Buddhists focus on being in the here and now.

Tibetan Buddhism, which developed into four distinct "schools," is rich in both history and practice. In addition to meditation, Tibetan Buddhists practice a number of rituals including the chanting of mantras and physical prostration. Reincarnation plays a major role in Tibetan Buddhism, where debts incurred in one life can be repaid in another.

When Gautama Buddha experienced his own enlightenment, he saw that he had lived many previous lives and taught that when we die we are reborn. However, for Buddhists, it is not the soul that is reborn, but rather our "consciousness" that exists on a continuum and moves from one life to the next.

Buddhists believe that what we experience today is a result of our actions in the past. We are responsible for those actions and there is no escape from the consequences. Karma, or the endless cycle of birth, death and rebirth, comes to an end only when we have reached Nirvana. Buddha wrote that the cycle of death and rebirth leads to the highest possible perfection.

> Him I call a Brahmana who has destroyed his doubts by knowledge and has plumbed the depth of the Eternal … Him I call a Brahmana who knows the mystery of death and rebirth of all beings, who knows his former lives, who is a sage of perfect knowledge and who has accomplished all that needs to be accomplished. – *The Dhammapada*

The Chinese yin-yang symbol represents all the opposite yet complementary forces in the universe – darkness and light; cold and heat; good and evil; life and death.
Neither can exist without its opposite.

CHAPTER 4

You and
Your Past Lives

You've inherited most from yourself,
not from your family. – Edgar Cayce

HAVE YOU EVER MET ANYONE that you seem to know a lot about, even though you've never met them before? A new brother-in-law? Your child's teacher?

 Are you drawn to visit or live in a place you've never seen? Spain? Kenya? Other periods of history that you feel you're aligned with, such as the Crusades or the French Revolution, even though you have no apparent connection to it?

 Have you had an affinity for a language that none of your family speaks or is not part of your known heritage? I know someone who was born and raised in Sault Ste Marie, a small town in Eastern Canada, who always had a desire to learn Japanese. He came to Toronto, not knowing any Japanese people, but found

I did not begin when I was born, nor when I was conceived. I have been growing, developing, through incalculable myriads of millenniums. All my previous selves have their voices, echoes, promptings in me. Oh, incalculable times again shall I be born.
– Jack London

someone with whom he could exchange language skills. He picked it up very quickly and now speaks it fluently. He is a blond-haired, blue-eyed, Japanese-speaking Canadian person.

∞ Have you always been fascinated by certain objects or music, such as Indian art or the violin, even though it hasn't got anything to do with your upbringing or family heritage?

∞ Is there a place, or are there places in the world that you absolutely dislike, even though you've never been there? Or repeatedly choose not to go there – like the basement of your house, or a hospital or doctor's office?

∞ Have you always wanted to climb Mt Everest even though you grew up on the plains of Saskatchewan or Minnesota?

∞ Is there an unusual scar or birthmark on your body that's unexplainable? That maybe even appeared during the first year after your birth?

∞ Have you had persistent phantom pain for as long as you can remember in any part of your body? A nagging ache around one eye, a sharp pain in a shoulder or a constant pain that comes and goes in exactly the same spot with no apparent reason?

So as through a glass darkly, the age long strife I see, where I fought in many guises, many names, but always me.
– General George S. Patton

∞ Have you had any fears since early childhood, with no explainable source? Green-backed turtles (and you've never, ever, seen one let alone been in the country they inhabit) or budgie birds, or goldfish?

∞ Do you have a recurring dream that's so vivid that you feel you're partly there all the time?

Then you've quite possibly experienced these phenomena in another lifetime.

Why Do We Choose the Lives We Choose?

To everything there is a season, and a time to every purpose under the heaven: a time to be born and a time to die; a time to plant, and a time to pluck up that which is planted; a time to kill, and a time to heal; a time to break down, and a time to build up; a time to weep, and a time to laugh; a time to mourn and a time to dance; a time to cast away stones, and a time to gather stones together; a time to embrace, and a time to refrain from embracing; a time to get, and a time to lose; a time to keep, and a time to cast away; a time to rend, and a time to sew; a time to keep silence, and a time to speak; a time to love, and a time to hate; a time of war, and a time of peace.

– Ecclesiastes 3:1

We choose the lives we live because of the lesson(s) we need to learn. Sometimes people have difficulty regressing into a past life because they have an issue or issues that need to be dealt with in the current lifetime before they can move back and explore other lifetimes. But in general, of the people in my experience who request past life regression – many of whom have never been hypnotized before – over 90% have traveled without difficulty into a past life regression.

Occasionally, when someone is curious about a particular interest they have – say, for instance, ancient Chinese block prints – and they decide they want to explore it further, their soul may decide that it is not the appropriate place for them to go first. It may take them somewhere else to learn the appropriate lessons before taking them to ancient China.

In the earliest recorded instance of the near death phenomenon, 731 AD, the historian Bede (c. 672 -735) wrote:

> *A man from the province of Northumbria returns from the dead ... "A handsome man in a shining robe was my guide ... He said to me ... 'You must now return to your body and live among men once more; but, if you will weigh your actions with greater care and study to keep your words and ways virtuous and simple, then when you die you too will win a home among these happy spirits that you see' ... I was most reluctant to return to my body ... but I did not dare to question my guide. Meanwhile, I know not how, I suddenly found myself alive among men once more." ... [I]nspired by an insatiable longing for the blessings of heaven, and by his words and by his life, he helped many people to salvation.*

– Bede, *History of the English Church and People*

There are times when clients come into the clinic for something that seems comparatively straight-forward; a fear of flying, or phobia around spiders for instance. When we start working with them in hypnosis to release this fear, they sometimes regress back to a past lifetime where the fear or phobia was installed. We use the healing process to clear it there, and when they return they are often amazed and sometimes disconcerted about the journey. Many of them say they didn't believe in past life before that experience. But the soul needed to take them there for the healing and wisdom, and that's where they went!

Past Life Regression: What It Is NOT

Past life regression is not a party game, nor is it something that's done by one person to another. A facilitator is someone who leads you into your past life. It's not necessary to be psychic or "special" or "weird" to be a facilitator or to experience past lives.

Reincarnation is not an exclusively Hindu or Buddhist concept, but it is part of the history of human origin. It is proof of the mindstream's capacity to retain knowledge of physical and mental activities. It is related to the theory of interdependent origination and to the law of cause and effect.
– The Dalai Lama

A psychic reading may or may not be accurate. A past life regression explores your experience. People occasionally come into the clinic and tell us, "I was told by someone that I lived another life as a healer (or a high priest)." This has nothing to do with past life regression. It's somebody else's interpretation of your energy.

Many clairvoyants can see past lives as they work with a client, but it is important to remember that the interpretation is theirs and not yours! An ethical clairvoyant will suggest you find a past life regression therapist so that you can personally experience the journey and gain the wisdom and healing it brings.

The vast majority of people experience past lives that may seem mundane or boring to the listener, but for the individual it may bring the answer they are seeking. I've never yet had a Cleopatra, Queen Elizabeth I or Leonardo Da Vinci, but I have had people who lived during those lifetimes and could record what they saw and felt about that person, from the slave, soldier or peddler's point of view. Each person's story is unique and special, whatever the role or name in that lifetime.

— • —

I once worked with a client who was convinced she had been Cleopatra and wanted past life regression to prove it. Because of the pre-decision on her part I was even more vigilant than usual in questioning and recording the journey. During the session I began asking questions she couldn't answer. She replied, "I'm not getting that information." She also missed out on some very important but little known data and could only come up with the highlights of Cleopatra's love life with Mark Anthony. Her body language was incongruent during the session, and so was the energy I received from her. Her language and voice were much too theatrical and aggressive.

In normal trance the client is almost motionless with REM (Rapid Eye Movement) apparent under the eyelids; the voice is usually low and, even when imperious, is more muted than usual. This client was physically animated – the whole experience was like a movie script being played out.

After the "Cleopatra" lifetime, while she was still relaxed, I deepened the hypnosis and took her into another lifetime in which she was an ordinary pioneer wife and mother. Her whole demeanor changed. Eye move-ment, breath, voice and diction lowered and slowed down. She gave off a relaxed and clean energy. When she came back to the sur-face, she was pleased about the Cleopatra event, but clearly and visibly moved by the pioneer story. I told her that I believed some-times a part of us wishes to have the

Reincarnation is making a comeback.
– on a lapel badge, Britain

attributes of a famous person so much, that we align ourselves subconsciously with that person. In NLP (neuro-linguistic programming) we call that modeling. But in past life journeys we understand it is a copy, not the real thing.

— • —

Reincarnation is not an idea dreamed up by those who wish to escape their fear of dying. It's not a quick way back to the land of the living, or an answer to our wish for immortality.

Whether a past life experience takes place in another time or another place, or whether it's a metaphor designed by your subconscious mind to allow you to experience healing or wisdom, past life regression gives us the opportunity for a new and clean start, another chance to learn and grow towards our goal of spiritual betterment.

Healing Ourselves

Past life memories come to us in many guises: déja-vu experiences, recurrent dreams, either of a specific location or a frightening event, a crippling phobia or unexplained, groundless fear. People who fear water, public speaking or heights (to name just a few common phobias) often uncover the memory of a death by drowning, hanging or burning at the stake, or falling from a high place. As these past life traumas are explored and resolved in therapy, the phobias cease to exist.

Emotional and physical challenges carried over from past incarnations into the present life can be quickly and effectively resolved through past life regression therapy in far fewer sessions than with conventional therapy. Many physical ailments are considered to be psychosomatic, and these conditions may diminish or cease altogether through past life regression therapy.

If we were locked into the patterns of emotion and thought that are set in place during our gestation, we would be prisoners of our history, controlled by a forgotten past. However, bringing our prebirth memories to consciousness through regression leads to a liberation from early negative experiences and to increased autonomy and freedom of choice. We can jettison our subconscious scripts. When the therapy is concluded, emotional limitations are lifted and the potential for personal fulfillment is increased. – Michael Gabriel, *Remembering Your Life Before Birth*

My hope is that you keep your mind open. It is not hypnotherapists who heal, it is you who have the ultimate responsibility. Past life regression and progression into future lives allow you to expand and explore your awareness and eliminate fear, anxiety, depression, and other negative tendencies, as well as the fear of death.
– Dr. Bruce Goldberg, *Past Lives, Future Lives*

Sylvia Browne, in the prologue to her book, *Past Lives, Future Healing*, tells of a man who underwent therapy of various kinds, including medication, for four years to deal with extreme panic and agoraphobia. Past life regression revealed that he had been poisoned in a past life and that his agoraphobia was triggered by an episode in a grocery store in which the word "poison" was used.

Psychiatrist Dr. Brian L. Weiss, author of *Many Lives, Many Masters*, tells a similar story of a patient of his who struggled for more than a year in conventional psychotherapy to get to the root of her many fears and phobias. Still severely impaired, she consented to try hypnosis in an attempt to discover if childhood traumas might be causing her problems. During one of these sessions, she regressed into a past life, much to the surprise of Dr. Weiss, and, after recalling events in other past lives, her symptoms began to dramatically improve. These sessions not only helped his patient, but they changed Dr. Weiss's life. He went on to do groundbreaking research in past life therapy.

> *As a therapist or a patient, you don't have to believe in past lives or reincarnation for past life therapy to work. The proof is in the pudding. As more than one fellow psychotherapist has said to me, "I still don't know if I believe in this past life stuff, but I use it, and it sure does work!"*
>
> – Dr. Brian Weiss, *Through Time Into Healing*

CHAPTER 5

Questions People Ask

I wonder what I was begun for, seeing as I am so soon done for. – Inscription on a gravestone of a little girl in Wales

Can we become other life forms?

Can we go to another life form, such as an animal or an element (wind, rain, etc.)? It is generally thought that animals have a universal soul or consciousness, but from time to time, I have experienced people taking on an animal shape or incarnation if they need to learn the lesson of that life. For instance, one of my clients became a snake and went through the skin-shedding process to learn that it was time for him to move into a new cycle in his current life. Another client briefly took the form of an eagle to learn that she had to move away from the minutiae of a relationship and into the wide view of the beauty and power of the world of the relationship. Many people who go on spiritual, psychic shamanic journeys take the form of an animal so that they may experience the wisdom that an animal can impart. And that includes becoming an element, like light or wind.

Can we come from or go to another planet?

Yes, we can, and do! Some of our clients and students have experienced lives on the ancient land masses of Atlantis and Lemuria. One in particular was on a red planet where he was a scientist who worked to prevent the planet from imploding on itself. But he learned that what he was trying to do was too little too late.

Can we live simultaneous lifetimes?

There are different points of view on this. I personally believe that we cannot. I believe that we have one soul, which from time to time may be fragmented through trauma, but it is just one soul living one life at a time. Each soul comes to this planet to experience the various lives it needs in order to progress.

How many past lives have I had?

There's no way of knowing. Just as there's no way of knowing how many you have yet to live. Every time we live a life, we live it to learn the experience and the wisdom, and if we don't learn the lesson, guess what? We do it again, to learn the same lesson, over and over, until we get it. Quantity is less important than quality of lives lived.

What about soul mates?

Many people believe that soul mates are the love of their life. My belief is that a soul mate is a soul that has been incarnated at the same approximate time as yours to help you uncover and discover parts of yourself in order to learn and heal in this lifetime. A soul mate can be a friend, a parent, a wife or husband or child. And the relationship may or may not be a kind or loving one.

What is the shortest time or average length of time between lives?

The turnaround can be as little as almost immediately to hundreds of years.

Will I experience pain in a past life?

You may travel in a lifetime where you are involved in a painful situation, for instance a battle or a violent death. But a trained facilitator should enable you to lift yourself above the pain so that you can watch or experience the event without the physical sensation, and receive the understanding without the pain.

How many past lives should I explore in a session?

If you are working with a facilitator, you may explore up to two lives in a single session. But if you are working by yourself without a facilitator, limit yourself to one past life per session.

Are there any negative aftereffects?

No, not if the journey is facilitated ethically, with kindness, following the ground rules set out in this book.

What about life between lives? Is there such a thing as life between lives?

Yes there is. It has many names, including Bardo. The name Bardo comes from the Tibetan understanding of death and reincarnation explained beautifully in the *Tibetan Book of the Dead*, a book about the plane of consciousness between earthly incarnations – lasting for a symbolic 49 days. Ancient Egyptians called it Amanthe, and the Australian Aborigines call it Angea. Ancient Hebrews called it Pardish. Many tribes and civilizations in the past prepared for that life between lives by burying a person's household goods with them when they died.

Life Between Life
(about Bardo)

Sometimes called the interlife, or Bardo, the life lived between physical incarnations is often a time of contemplation and learning. It is the time when the soul reviews the life just past and prepares itself for the next incarnation. Those souls who have failed to learn the lessons or overcome the challenges in a succession of lives, often choose to place themselves in similar situations, sometimes again and again, until the lesson is learned or the challenge is overcome.

Bardo, as defined in the *Tibetan Book of the Dead*, consists of three stages. In the first stage, a bright light – the light of higher consciousness – is perceived by the soul entity. In the second stage, the soul entity must struggle (usually unsuccessfully) with the beliefs of the life just lived and insight into the spiritual nature of being. This then leads to the third stage, the rebirth of the soul into another life and the living out of the karmic script.

Some consider the life between lives to be our "natural home," a plane of consciousness filled with lightness and love, which we leave in order to continue our journey of soul learning. In the interlife, we learn that our spiritual essence remains when the physical being dies. There have been many descriptions and physical depictions of the interlife, but it is a timeless and "placeless" dimension, perceived by and accessed by the subconscious mind.

> Life between death and a new birth is as rich and varied as life here between birth and death.
> – Rudolf Steiner

In the *Tibetan Book of the Dead* it is described as a place where :

> ... *[Y]ou have no physical body of flesh and blood, so whatever sounds, colors and rays of light occur, they cannot hurt you and you cannot die ... know this to be the bardo state.*

It is the place that some regression therapists, including Edgar Cayce, call "the Blue Mist." During past life regression sessions at the clinic, we refer to the Blue Mist as the life between lives, an area of peace, wisdom and healing. We enable some of our clients to go into the Bardo, or Blue Mist, state to help them understand the purpose and work of this current lifetime – why they chose to come into this life in their current form, and why they chose the country, family and focus of this life.

To Those Who Debunk Past Life Regression, I Say ...

Unless there is a gigantic conspiracy involving thirty university departments all over the world, and several hundred respected scientists in various fields ... the only conclusion the unbiased observer can come to must be that there does exist a small number of people who obtain knowledge, existing either in other people's minds or in the outer world, by means as yet unknown to science.

– Prof. Hans J. Eysenck

The ultimate answer to the skeptic is, "Try it."

When I experience with my own eyes and ears someone change the way they look and sound, their demeanor, their thinking and thought processes, I have to appreciate that this physical and mental transformation is coming from somewhere. To me it doesn't matter what the "debunkers" say. The other night I was watching the moon and, in time, clouds covered it over. But that doesn't mean the moon wasn't there, just because I couldn't see it. In Canada, during the long, gray days of winter, we don't see the sun for long periods, but that doesn't mean it isn't up there. And I can hear you saying, right now ... but we *know* it's up there ... it's been scientifically proven, that even if clouds cover the sun or the moon, it's still there!

Well, I have news for you! Scientists are proving, through research, by tracking down lives that people have described, that we do seem to go to other places, other lifetimes. There are recorded

The prevailing
orthodoxy is
when your brain
dies your mind
perishes also.
That is so deeply
believed that
scientists fail to
understand it is
an assumption
only and there is
no reason why
aspects of the
mind should not
survive death of
the brain.
— Dr. Ian
Stevenson

cases of children who say to their mother and father, "You are not my parents," and they then name their "real" parents. This is something that can, and has been proven repeatedly, and in numerous cultures and countries.

Have you never observed that children will sometimes, of a sudden, give utterance to ideas which makes us wonder how they got possession of them? Which presuppose a long series of other ideas and secret self-communings? Which break forth like a full stream out of the earth, an infallible sign that the stream was not produced in a moment from a few raindrops, but had long been flowing concealed beneath the ground?

— J.G. Herder, German pastor and philosopher

Dr. Ian Stevenson of the University of Virginia has documented more than 2,000 cases of children who appear to have had experience of reincarnation. Some of these very young children have demonstrated the ability to speak a foreign language they had never heard, and have known details of towns and families they had never been to, and that happened before they were born. Were these children tapping into a collective unconscious or a "stream of knowledge" that included past events, symbols and history, or did they gain their knowledge from past lives?

Dr. Stevenson believed that by working with children there was less chance of "contamination" of memory through access to information by reading, exposure to images or overheard conversations. Perhaps the most famous case of past life memory in a child is that of Shanti Devi, an eight-year-old girl born in Delhi, India. In 1935, Shanti claimed that she was once a housewife named

Lugdi Devi who had lived in Mathura, in northern India, and had died in childbirth. Shanti began speaking of her "other life" at the age of three. When she was taken to the village of Mathura in 1935, she went straight to the house where Lugdi had lived, and was able to identify her relatives, including her husband's brother and father. She also dug up items that she had buried in the previous lifetime! All of this information had been documented before Shanti went to the village, and none of it has ever been refuted.

CHAPTER 6

How It Works

Allow yourself the possibility of being surprised
by an unexpected experience. Often, these are
the ones that induce the most growth.
– Brian Weiss, *Through Time Into Healing*

IF YOU'RE CONSIDERING the possibility of
taking the journey into a past life, perhaps you'd
like to know a little more about how it feels, and
what it's like to go on this journey.

The past life is usually accessed by allowing the
mind to go into the subconscious (alpha state)
and then into the superconscious. This can be
done through hypnosis, meditation or other
mind-expanding techniques. Some people may
find that they are able to go into this state if they
have a massage with a therapist who works with
energy.

Spirit is the pure
essence, the God
force and the
spark of God –
consciousness is
one fragment of
that Totality.
– William J.
Baldwin

Dr. Brian Weiss, in *Through Time Into Healing*,
writes of going to a shiatsu therapist for treatment
of chronic back and neck pain. During the sessions
he would meditate, and in the third session he
reached a state of deep relaxation. He records:

"As the therapist was working on my feet, I was startled by an awareness of a scene from another time. I was awake, not sleeping. I knew where my body was, but I was watching and re-experiencing a movie beyond my mind.

"In this scene, I was taller and thinner, with a small, dark, pointed beard ... Looking into the eyes of this thin man, I knew that I was this person. I felt his emotions. I could see through his eyes."

Some people experience the life by seeing it as if they're watching a movie or appearing in the movie. Others sense that they are there and are totally immersed in the experience itself, not actually seeing anything. Others hear or simply know that they're there. Once you've learned to trust what comes up without letting the conscious mind question or criticize, the process begins to flow, from one scene to another, or one event to another.

Sometimes it makes very little sense while it's happening, but afterwards, you realize that if indeed you were that child in 6th-century Ireland, or somewhere hot and sandy in 4 BC, you may not have known how to read or the name of the place where you lived, or even the name of the food you were eating. It's just what you were accustomed to. Being able to discuss and evaluate the experience with a facilitator often helps piece together the puzzling parts of a past lifetime.

Our spirit minds remember every moment our souls have experienced, in this life and every other life we've lived since we were created ... And so by accessing those cell memories, we can rid ourselves of long-buried illness, phobias, pain, and trauma.
– Sylvia Browne, *Past Lives, Future Lives*

Soul and Spirit

The soul comes from
without into the human
body, as into a temporary
abode, and it goes out of it
anew ... it passes into
other habitations, for the
soul is immortal.

– Ralph Waldo Emerson

The terms soul and the spirit are often used interchangeably, but they are different. According to various teachers, the soul is deep within us, immortal, and a part of our "self." It passes from body to body, or life to life, acquiring the experience and lessons of each life. The spirit, on the other hand, is the vital essence or animating force within all living things.

More About
How It Works

Past life regression works by taking us into the Alpha state, bypassing the critical conscious mind, going from the subconscious into the superconscious, which connects with the soul and the universal energy. Someone might tell me they're in a marketplace, and I'll ask them what they see. They'll tell me they can't see, they just "know" because they can feel the hustle and bustle around them. Or, in some cases, they can hear or smell what's going on. Most people tell me they can "see" the marketplace in great detail, including the sound of people's voices, the smell of the food, the sounds and smells of animals.

The past is the future, the future is the past ... It all gives me a headache!
– Captain Kathryn Janeway, *Star Trek: Voyager*

Perhaps our more primitive capability, our largely unused right brain, is beginning to function again as it so often does in less "civilized" societies. Perhaps this "metaphoric mind" can come to know a universe which is nonlinear, in which the terms time and space have very different meanings ... And every time new forces or energies have been discovered in our universe, they have changed our perception of reality and have opened new doors and new opportunities for the human being. – Carl Rogers

What If I Don't See Anything?

You can't
depend on your
eyes if your
imagination is
out of focus
– Mark Twain

There are times when people claim they can't see anything, and so they don't think they are anywhere. We're so trained to observe and "see" things (in order to believe them) that some people are disappointed and believe the process isn't working. But the reality may be that they are experiencing life inside a cave at a time where there was no available light at night, or possibly this is the life of a blind person.

Many people "feel" where they are, or just "know." They'll say, "I sense I'm in a marketplace and I can hear the sounds of voices." We must be open to exploring the experience from all angles and possibilities so that it's possible to move through the life.

You can observe
a lot just by
watching
– Yogi Berra

Sometimes a person may have come into a life as a very young baby, and find they can't see or say much because they are as yet unable to see or speak. So it may be necessary to move them ahead in the life to a time when they are aware enough to begin to tell the story.

There is also something called the law of "reverse effect." You may simply be trying too hard to see or sense something.

> *The harder you try to do something, the less likely it is that you will succeed ... If you are trying too hard, you are not relaxing enough to allow the powerful subconscious to do the work for you. Your tense and anxious effort sends an unspoken message to the subconscious that there is fear of failure, which then tends to realize itself.*
> – Ted Andrews, *How to Uncover Your Past Lives*

CHAPTER 7

Preparing
For Your Journey

Even the memory of a past life came to him occasionally, almost like a dream. He looked at a passing stranger, and felt that somewhere he must have lived a life of joy with him.
– Walt Whitman

HYPNOSIS CAN BE DESCRIBED AS FOCUSED concentration in an altered state. Your conscious mind remains active; you are aware of your surroundings at all times; and you are in complete control of what happens. Your subconscious mind can also be accessed through meditation or a light trance, and that is often enough for past life regression. However, there is a difference between hypnosis and meditation, as Henry Bolduc explains in *Life Patterns*:

> "*The levels are the same, alpha and theta, but there is a difference. In meditation, we generally open ourselves to guidance coming to us at the conscious level from a higher level of consciousness, the subconscious or superconscious. Symbolically, we open ourselves to guidance and to inspiration from our own higher mind, which is an eternal and everlasting source.*

"In [hypnosis], we focus the conscious mind and use it as a tool to instruct and to guide the unconscious in the directions that we consciously want our lives to go. The difference lies in how we use the alpha and theta levels, and not in the levels themselves. Meditation can be likened to a telescope looking out into the vastness of space.

"Hypnosis can be symbolized by a microscope focusing in on a specific goal or objective."

The important thing to remember is that by accessing our past lives, we can begin to see the patterns that exist beyond the time and place we are now living in. This knowledge can help us make responsible choices both in our actions and in our behavior.

It is possible to access past lives through self-hypnosis, or you may feel more comfortable undertaking the journey with a qualified facilitator. There are advantages and disadvantages to both approaches.

Benefits of Doing It for Yourself

1. Convenience of time and place – you can experience past life regression in your home, at a time (or times) of your own choosing
2. Cost – there will be no cost, other than purchasing a tape recorder, microphone and tapes
3. Frequency of sessions – although I recommend you visit one past life during each session, there is no limit to the number of sessions you may have
4. Privacy – no one else need hear or see you experience your past lives

Disadvantages of Doing It for Yourself

1. Too much conscious awareness, inability to let go and relax – you may have trouble quieting your mind or reaching a state of relaxation without the help of a facilitator
2. Difficult to process yourself out of situations of discomfort, fear, etc. – you will have to be prepared to lead yourself out of a frightening or violent situation (see point #5 under **Environment**, page 57)
3. Household interruptions such as phone, pets, outside noises, etc. – it's important not to be interrupted in the middle of a session
4. Less deep state of hypnosis – although a light trance is often sufficient, you may find that you need assistance in reaching an effective depth of hypnosis for your session; everybody's different
5. No opportunity for immediate feedback or verification – it's useful to be able to talk about a past life and the feelings around it once the session is over

My life often seemed to me like a story that has no beginning and no end. I had the feeling that I was an historical fragment, an excerpt for which the preceding and succeeding text was missing. I could well imagine that I might have lived in former centuries and there encountered questions I was not yet able to answer; that I had been born again because I had not fulfilled the task given to me.
– Carl Jung

Benefits of Having a Facilitator

1. Led by a trained, certified professional – you may feel safer knowing that a qualified person is in the room with you
2. Deeper state of hypnosis – a facilitator will recognize whether or not you are in a sufficient state of trance to regress into a past life
3. A helping hand in times of trouble – again, you may feel safer on your journey if you know someone is there to lead you out of a difficult situation
4. Uninterrupted, discrete space for the journey – a qualified facilitator will be able to provide the appropriate environment for a past life journey
5. Professional, ethical structure to achieve fullest wisdom and forgiveness – a facilitator will help you close off the past life and also help you to understand the wisdom of the past life

Disadvantages of Having a Facilitator

1. Cost – you will have to pay for the session and costs can vary
2. Lack of convenience – you may have to travel some distance and you will have to book an appointment
3. Possibility for personality conflict – finding a compatible hypnotist is no different than finding a compatible therapist or doctor; you need to feel comfortable with them and trust their wisdom and experience

Do It Yourself!

Beginning Your Own Journey

Pre-session
1. Before you begin your pre-session, you will want to pre-record both your
   - Invocation script, and
   - Regression script
2. Decide when you want to take the journey. You'll need a full hour or more of uninterrupted time.
3. Decide on the focus of your journey.
4. Decide if a trusted, silent friend will accompany you on your journey.

Environment
1. Turn off all phones.
2. Find a quiet place where you won't be interrupted by children, neighbors or pets – human or otherwise!
3. If recording (remember, you have to talk out loud to yourself if you're going to record) make sure you have a microphone very close by (I suggest a lapel mike), and a recording device you can easily activate.
4. You'll need at least an hour for your session.
5. Prepare yourself to handle a difficult or frightening situation. I recommend that you create an "anchor" for yourself that will bring you back into your body enough so that you feel safe while you continue your journey to its closure.

∞ For example, rub your thumb and index finger together in a circular motion; or link the fingers of both hands together. Use a physical gesture of some kind that will work for you without being too disruptive or invasive. It should be something

> The art of self hypnosis concerns timing, tone, and delivery – not going too fast or too slow, being too forceful or too meek. The inner mind responds very differently from the conscious mind. It contains profound depth and wisdom, yet, it works slowly and requires clear, simple questions or instructions.
> – Henry Bolduc, *Life Patterns*

that will bring you into enough awareness that you will recognize that you are in the here and now. Practice this gesture beforehand, so that your subconscious mind will recognize the signal if you need to use it.

Remember that you are in the here and now and are just visiting a past life. You must disassociate from the feelings of fear and any uncomfortable sensations you are experiencing. You can "watch" the experience as if you were watching a movie. You *must* finish the life, however; you can't leave it unfinished simply because you are afraid or uncomfortable. If you don't, the danger is that you might bring the pain or discomfort with you into your current life. To avoid this, close the life off with forgiveness, compassion and wisdom. And then drop the curtain and move through the life between lives to the current day.

If You're Using a Facilitator

1. Choose the facilitator you wish to work with very carefully, using the Code of Conduct in the Addenda of this book as a guide.
2. Verify that they have been trained in the skills and wisdom of past life regression.
3. When you call, ask if you may speak to other people they have worked with and/or the facilitator directly so that you get a sense of who they are and how they work.
4. Ask if they record the session and whether you should bring a tape with you.
5. Find out the fees charged and the duration of the session.
6. Prepare yourself by thinking about what you would like to get out of the session: what you want to know, what you want to find out.
7. Spend a few moments before you go into your session by relaxing and promising yourself you'll have a relaxed, interesting, profound journey.
8. You'll want to feel relaxed, so no coffee before the session!

What It Does for You

Past-life therapy helps people to be more balanced and responsible, to gain emotional and spiritual maturity and a sense of their true worth. In some cases, the recall and therapy is so vibrant that it is like a total and complete spiritual release, followed by profound peace.
– Henry Bolduc,
The Journey Within

Past life regression helps you understand your life issues and where you stand in this current lifetime.

✔ It can release chronic pain or illness such as asthma or psoriasis.

✔ It can help you deal with psychological distress such as anxiety, sadness or panic attacks.

✔ It can give you a sense of your life's purpose at this time, on this planet.

✔ It can bring understanding about repeated patterns in this current life.

✔ It can help bring some understanding and joy into a current life that is seemingly dark and depressing.

✔ It gives you a greater perspective of who you are and who you could be and your connection to the universe.

✔ It helps explain things that you thought were unexplainable.

✔ It helps you find the true person inside of yourself – the one you haven't recognized.

✔ It helps you understand your connection, your relationship, to your parents, your siblings, and the others you are close to. Why did you marry the person you married? Why are your children like you, or not like you? Why are you like or not like your own birth parents?

How Past Life Regression Helped Me

Where the sun always shines
There's a desert below
It takes a little rain
To make love grow.

– Oak Ridge Boys, *It Takes a Little Rain (to Make Love Grow)*

There was a time when I suffered from severe migraine headaches on the left side of my head, just behind my eye, and they'd spread all the way to the back of my head, gripping it like a vice. I went for vitamin therapy and for a while they subsided but never really went away. Then they became unbearably severe again. One day, when I was taking one of Henry Bolduc's classes, a past life regression led me into the life of a woman in what looked and felt like medieval England. I lived by myself in a cave on the side of a hill. I was a witch or a crone. I was so dirty I could smell myself! My hair was filthy and matted. I was quite disgusting. I was very much an outcast and people used to leave me bits of food so that I could survive and work for them.

My role, my job, was to help women in the village give birth to their babies, and also to give abortions. At one point, I had helped a woman deliver a baby girl during a very difficult birthing, but the woman died. Her husband was so infuriated that he came storming into my cave with a huge rock. He smashed in my skull with the rock and I died. Under hypnosis, I was able to forgive him and leave the pain behind in that life. Since then, I've had no migraines.

We don't receive wisdom; we must discover it for ourselves after a journey that no one can take for us.
– Marcel Proust

Questions You May Want to Ask Yourself

We seem to travel in "pods," by which I mean, your daughter in this lifetime may have been an aunt or a close friend in another, or your mother in this lifetime could have been your husband in a previous lifetime. A woman who came to the clinic seeking relief from anxiety and depression discovered that her current husband was the alcoholic father who had caused the fire that disfigured her face in that lifetime.

Before you begin your past life regression you may want to prepare yourself by thinking about some of the following questions:

? Do I have a specific purpose for this particular journey?

? What is it?

? How will I recognize my soul mate or mates in this lifetime?

? How will I know when I'm making the right decision?

? What do I need to understand to help me release myself from the pattern or habit of _____?

? How can I prepare myself or a loved one to leave this life?

? I need guidance in my choice of a life partner. How do I obtain that?

? What do I need to understand in order to learn to trust?

? Why did I choose my parents?

? Why did I choose the role I have in my current lifetime?

? What parts of myself am I ignoring in this lifetime?

CHAPTER 8

Steps To The Regression Process

Do you know at this very moment you are
surrounded by eternity? And do you know
that you can use that eternity if you so desire?
– Don Juan (Carlos Castaneda)

THE FOLLOWING PROCESS grew out of that
taught by Henry Bolduc in *The Journey Within*.

There are 14 basic steps to each past life
regression journey. Each step flows into the next.
The depth level of hypnosis varies with each
individual as does the pace and timing. Each
person responds according to his or her own
temperament, style and experience.

∞ Hypnosis or Self-Hypnosis – entering your
own relaxed, receptive, 100% natural level
of mind

∞ Auric protection and soul permission for
the journey through time

∞ The journey back through time beyond
the womb

∞ Blue Mist Experience – the time in between lives – Bardo.

∞ Past-Life Regression – using all your senses in the re-experiencing of stored memories

∞ Open-ended questions are asked during the regression. For example, "What happens next?" or "What's happening now?" and you relate your experiences to the facilitator or into your microphone. Sometimes you may receive a wealth of information, other times it may take a while to really "be" there. The more you do it, the more associated – or involved – you become. When you start you may find that you get only glimpses of someone who may or may not be you ... but as you progress, you become that person, with all of your senses.

∞ Death Experience – a safe and positive way to complete the life's memory. You rise above the body, and send love and compassion as part of the closing of that lifetime.

∞ Soul Lessons – you are asked what you gained from the life, the wisdom, its lessons, the reasons, talents, etc.

∞ Forgiveness – also called "Healing the Past"– you mentally look into the eyes of yourself and everyone from that life and send love and forgiveness to them. You bless them, release them and let them fade.

- Return through the Blue Mist – bringing back with you something special, understanding, awareness, and perhaps recognition of patterns

- Protective Suggestions – that you will retain in your conscious mind only that which is important, helpful and beneficial

- Return to Present – stepping firmly into the present in fullness of strength

- Wake-up Procedure – a process for total normalization and well-being

- Discussion and Evaluation of Session – the time to evaluate, document and discuss what has transpired

The journey within is a sacred experience – a vision quest – to the center of your being. The journey is personal and different for everyone. You do not have to answer or explain yourself to anyone – you can evaluate your results for yourself, then accept the validity of your own experience.

Taking Yourself on The Journey

Now that you're ready for the journey, what's the next step? Because you are opening up your energy field, you need to make sure that you surround yourself with light and a prayer or invocation to whatever or whoever you believe protects you. The following invocation is one that I, and others in our clinic, use and find very powerful. It will keep you feeling safe and connected – sort of like travel insurance! Take a few minutes to connect yourself and those you love with the light before starting on the adventure. It's a lovely ritual. Allow yourself the time to experience this part of the journey.

Recording Your Invocation and Script

Use a tape that runs for at least 60 minutes, or, better still, 90 minutes. Speak very slowly into your microphone and wherever there are pauses (…) in the script, allow enough time for the subconscious mind to absorb the information and your answers to be formulated and spoken.

Invocation [record all of the following]
Calling on Spirit, my guides, the God of my belief and understanding, [Jesus, Buddha, Mary, or whoever or whatever you choose] *to protect and heal me as I take this journey of the Soul with integrity and respect. From the light of God, may the Guides or angels who accompany me on my journey be of 100% pure light and may I journey within the safety of pure light. May I be guided to other times and other places that will give clear insight and understanding about the current lifetime and allow the wisdom and learning to be brought forward into this time and this place so that I may live in pure light.*

[continue recording]
Now become aware of the bubble of white light forming around you about 12 inches away from your body. This white light keeps you focused and safe for the journey ahead.

Script [record all of the following]
Before you start, do whatever you need to do to make yourself comfortable. Move your legs, your arms, your head to make sure that you are in the best possible place so that you can relax and enjoy that relaxation.

Now that you are ready, just look forward or upward and focus on a spot on the ceiling. I am going to count down slowly from ten to one. With every descending number, just slowly blink your eyes, as if in slow motion, with each number.

Ten ... that's good, nice and slowly.

*Nine, that's good ... eight (2 second pause) ...
seven (2 second pause) ... six (2 second pause) ...
five (2 second pause) ... four (2 second pause) ...
three (2 second pause) ... two (2 second pause) ...
and one.*

Now you can just close your eyes. Right now, in your eyelids, there may be a feeling of relaxation, or a comfortable tired feeling. Whatever the feeling is, just allow that to multiply, to magnify, and to become greater. This is something that you do; nobody else can do it for you. So just take your time now ... and .... relaaaaaaaax .... there may be movement starting in your eyelids, and that's perfectly OK. .... These movements are called REM, or rapid eye movements and they are a perfectly natural part of this experience.

*Just allow that feeling of relaxation that is now in your eyelids, to move outward, as in imaginary waves or ripples, to your entire face .... .and neck ....
outwards and downwards .... moving down to*

your shoulders .... easily, gently, smoothly relaxing down your upper arms .... your lower arms .... your hands .... and even your fingers relax .... relax all the way .... down ....

Take a deep breath now and let your lungs fill with relaxation. Allow that relaxation to flow to your stomach, to your spine, and slowly down your spine to your hips, to your legs and feel it, all the way out to your toes, filling your entire body with relaxation. Now, just slow down a little bit and mentally examine your entire body. If there is any area that is not completely relaxed, just allow that part to catch up and to become as relaxed as the rest of you.

Pause for a few seconds.

Now allow yourself to slow down just a little bit more .... then a bit more. I am going to count downward once again from ten to one. This time with every descending number, just allow yourself to slow down and follow your breathing .... each out breath, becoming more still, more centered, with every number, and at the count of one, you can enter your own deep level of relaxation .... counting down and following your breath .... now: ten, nine, eight, seven, six, five, four, three, two, one.

You are now at your own natural level of relaxation and from this level you may move to any other level with complete awareness. You are in complete control at every level of your mind. This is something that you have chosen to do. It is here and it is now.

Pause for a few seconds.

Now begin by comparing your mind to the surface of a quiet pond. On the surface everything looks peaceful and still, but below the surface there is great depth where much is happening. You can think of my voice as a breeze whispering in the trees along the shore.

Not everyone realizes his or her full capacities, and you have to discover those capacities in whatever way you wish. One of the things I would like for you to discover is that your own subconscious mind can listen to me and also deal with something at the same time. Perhaps you can remember doing this as a child in school, gazing out the window while the teacher was talking. (Pause.) Or walking with a friend and talking to that friend at the same time. Two separate things, yet happening at the same time. Your subconscious is here and can hear every word, so why bother having to think or to move about or to make any sort of effort? You are in a place where you can let go safely, and just relax.

You may take a deep breath now, and you will notice that a drifting might occur. You may feel light, you may feel heavy, or you may feel that your body is asleep, although your mind is alert. There is less and less importance to be attached to my voice, and more and more significance to be given to your own inner reality, to your own inner experience.

Stored deep in your subconscious are wonderful memories of other times and other places. Your subconscious can call upon and access those memories, memories you only thought you had misplaced. Experiences you only thought you had mislaid.

By looking deeply into the recesses of your mind, you can see your vision and hear the voice of your heart. With this insight, comes new growth and new understanding. On your return to the here and now you can apply this knowledge to understand yourself and your world better. In a moment we will start the process which will lead you into the recall of memories.

(Pause)

Imagine now that you are inside the most beautiful room.......this room may be one that you have seen before or it may be one that you are imagining right now......either way... it is the most beautiful room ..... beautiful, peaceful and comfortable......your room... your very own beautiful room......... you feel so good, surrounded by all this beauty ... You realize you feel safe and very peaceful.

Take a look around and notice how it's furnished, what's on the floor, the colors and textures.... and suddenly you realize that it is completely round ... Walk around the room ... Acclimatize yourself to it ...

(Long pause)

And as you wander around the room, you notice there's a large full-length mirror in the center of this beautiful room.

Step over to it ... Look into the mirror and see your own reflection ... Notice how good you look when you are relaxed and feeling in control ... And as you look, become aware that your image is slowly dissolving ... There's a swirling of color and mist ... beautiful colors ... swirling around.......the colors blending and separating......the colors become a mist......a soft......blue mist ...and the mist slowly clears ...

You see a shape taking form inside the mist ... And then you see yourself emerging – say five or ten years ago – in a happy time ... A reflection of you ... really happy ... you remember what you were doing then to make you so happy ... The image is so strong that you try to reach out to touch it ... and as you do ... it shifts ... and dissolves ... and other images come ... from different happy times in your life ... maybe at school ... maybe playing with friends when you were a child ... Notice the clothes... notice who is with you ...

With each memory, with each vision, you relax deeper and deeper ... As you watch and become absorbed in

*the good times you see in the mirror, you know that
this mirror is showing you what has helped shape the
you that you are now ... and with each reflection ...
and each dissolving of that reflection, you go deeper
and deeper ... and further back ... further back ...
further back ... into your memory ...*

*And as you look into the mirror again ... it is filled
with swirling colors once more... .... misty shapes
appearing and disappearing in the mist ... colors
swirling ... appearing and disappearing ... as you feel
changes within yourself as you find yourself traveling
back ... back in time ... back into another part of you
... another time ... another place ... and you feel
yourself going deeper and deeper into relaxation ...*

*Be in touch with your feelings, begin to be in touch
with the part of you that asks for understanding......that wants to know more......... Because
there is a part of you that really yearns for
understanding ... for reconciliation ... for a
broadening of awareness ...... begin to feel a shift now
...a shift in feeling...... a shift in seeing ... It's almost
as if you begin to walk through another dimension of
time and space.*

*Feel your mind expanding down into your
subconscious ... out into your superconscious ......
expanding like the circles in a pond when you drop in
a pebble. Your mind expands ... and expands ...
bringing into the conscious self that wonderful
knowledge and information ... that is available to you
... about the totality of who you truly are.*

*And as you move towards a time that gives you
wisdom and understanding ... out of the colors ... out
of the mist ... within the mirror ... a shape is forming
... vague and soft ... you feel safe and comfortable ...
you feel more relaxed than ever as the colors swirl and
the shape begins to sharpen ...*

And you watch as the image you see in the mirror, the shape, mimics your movements ... and you realize this image is you ... but from another time ... and another place ... and as the mist clears ... and the shape becomes clearer and sharper ... and ... as it clears and sharpens ... you go down deeper and deeper in to relaxation ... feeling safe ... feeling secure ...... watching the mirror ... seeing the shape become clear ... seeing what is happening now in the mirror ...

Speak out loudly and say what you perceive.

Are you male or female? ...

About how old? ...

What are you wearing? ...

Is anyone with you? ...

Are you inside or outside? ...

Is it daytime or nighttime?

Going slowly up your body, note what you are wearing. How does it look or feel? Feel the texture, see the colors. Say out loud what you perceive. How do you feel?

Do you have anything on your head? What is the color of your hair?

Do you have anything in your hands?

Speak out loud and tell the story of what is going on. What is happening around you?

Now, in your mind's eye, slowly look around the place where you are standing and say out loud what you see. Look around and talk about what you perceive. Just let the story tell itself.

Describe your home or dwelling place. How does it feel?

And now, you may look for other people, or a time when you feel yourself near or with other people. Talk out loud about the people, your impressions and feelings. Perhaps there is someone special, someone with whom you have a close bond, an affinity or a strong connection.

Now, look for some vehicle of transportation, something you might have ridden on or in, something that feels familiar when you sit in or on it. Talk out loud about anything that you or others are using for transportation.

At this time you might also wish to taste something that you are eating. What are you eating? Can you smell the food cooking? Can you taste it? Talk out loud about this.

Now, if you listen carefully, you may hear your own name being spoken by a friend or someone calling out to you. What do they call you?

What is your work or profession? What are you learning?

Now, move to the time of an important event in your life – a significant episode.

(Pause)

Talk out loud about what is happening. What do you see or feel? What sounds do you hear? What smells do you notice? Remember to let the story tell itself.

Move now to the next important event or another significant time in that life.

(Pause)

What is happening now? What are you doing?

You may move now to the circumstances and the events that led to your death, and to the death experience itself. Detach yourself from any physical pain or discomfort, but note the events and the death *experience itself. Talk out loud about what is happening and what you do.*

As you pass from that life, lift yourself up above, and look down on the body you left behind........notice what is happening there and who is with you. Send compassion and love to that person below you...........and send forgiveness for any pain caused, knowingly or unknowingly. Look also into the eyes of everyone you saw, those you have loved, that person who was special to you – and send love and forgiveness, for any pain caused, knowingly or unknowingly. And as you do this important step, you bless them and send them forgiveness ...

From this higher perspective, what were the lessons you learned from this life? How did you gain? How did you grow?

What brought you to the greatest happiness or the greatest fulfillment in the life?

What did you learn or accomplish in that life that can help in your present life?

In light of those new discoveries and understanding, please relay a message from your past-life self to your present-life self. What does your past-life self wish to communicate to the present-life self?

What task or activity could you perform in your current life that would help to heal and to balance that memory?

(Pause)

Bless that past life part of you and let it fade. And those you loved in that life, and those you loved less, release them, let them fade. As they fade, let them go as they bless and forgive you. Let the veil slowly drop. Allow the curtain to close slowly. Allow a full healing of that life and that time. Take all the time that you wish – and when they have faded, you may continue.

Close of Session:

Now you start your journey back...........going to that timeless place in a placeless time where all things are revealed clearly to you

Now, as you prepare for the journey back, you will bring back with you only that which is helpful and beneficial. Bring back something holy or special – a gem of wisdom, but only what you want. You may release other feelings, memories, or impressions now, and retain in your conscious mind only that which is important, helpful and beneficial for you to retain at this time.

Now, slowly you return through the Blue Mist, traveling on the avenue of the heart, where all things are revealed to you, through that warm and safe place where nothing can harm you – returning through levels of your mind and bringing back the information that you have recorded. Slowly come back through the years into what we call the present life, the present day and location.

And as you return, realize that you have done very well. You have opened in trust and thankfulness. In a little while, there will be a count to ten....at the number ten, reorient yourself fully into the present, so that at the count of ten, you will be wide awake, refreshed, feeling better than you have felt in a long, long time.

One, stepping firmly and fully into the present time.

Two, feel total normalization at every level of your being.

Three, feel the life energies returning to your extremities.

Four, You may wish to move your hands, feet or neck.

Five, remembering what you have accomplished.

Six, realizing how you have done so very well.

Seven, coming up now to your full awareness.

Eight, re-energizing.

Nine, revitalized, and

Ten, slowly open your eyes, back into this time and this space. Wide awake. Welcome back!

Follow-up Suggestions

If you're being facilitated, it's a good idea to make notes with your facilitator or by yourself when you get home. Use the Memories Chart in the Addenda to track your lives so that you can see the similarities and the patterns between them.

Patterns

Charting your lives will help you recognize the similarities and links between them. Begin to think about the patterns that you see repeated in your past lives and your present life to find the questions that need to be answered, the issues that need to be addressed in this lifetime. Make connections. Here are some behavior patterns to look for:

- Adventure and pioneering
- Anger or rage
- Avoidance
- Beneficial partnerships
- Bigotry or prejudice
- Courage
- Creativity
- Education and learning
- Enjoying nature and the outdoors
- Entertaining and bringing joy
- Feelings of abandonment
- Greed or ill will
- Healing and teaching
- Illness

- Indifference or non-involvement
- Loyalty
- Mistrust
- The need for solitude
- The need to feel safe and secure
- Nurturing and caring
- Rejection
- Self-sacrifice
- Spirituality and piety
- Suffering
- Thrill-seeking and danger
- Victimization
- Violence
- Working with children

We occasionally stumble over the truth, but most of us pick ourselves up and hurry on as if nothing happened.
– Anonymous

CHAPTER 9

What Happens Next?

Sometimes you have to play for a long time to be able to play like yourself – Miles Davis

SOMETIMES, WHETHER YOU ARE with a facilitator or by yourself, the first life you experience appears very sketchy or vague, or you feel disassociated from it, as if it were someone else. But, as with anything, the more you do it, the better you become at it. So the next time, and the time after that, the experience will be stronger, more clear. You'll feel associated and the sensation will be very near and real.

Explore the River of the Soul; whence or in what order you have come.
– Zoroaster

Deepak Chopra, in *How to Know God*, suggests that we think of reincarnation and former lives as an issue of awareness. As we open up our minds and increase our awareness, we enter a whole new realm of possibilities. We are no longer confined by the limitations of the physical world:

> *"There is much evidence that the mind is not confined by time and space … Just as a quantum of energy can leap between two points*

without crossing the space in between, so apparently can a thought. A field of awareness flows in, around, and through each of us … When you see a familiar face, your brain doesn't run through its catalog of all known faces to arrive at who your friend is … what we call recognition takes place instantly, at a deeper level of consciousness."

Using the Outcomes in Your Present Life

"You know," said Arthur, "it's at times like this, when I'm trapped in a Vogon airlock with a man from Betelgeuse, and about to die from asphyxiation in deep space that I really wish I'd listened to what my mother told me when I was young."
"Why, what did she tell you?"
"I don't know, I didn't listen."

– Douglas Adams, *The Hitchhiker's Guide to the Galaxy*

Take the wisdom that you've brought from your past life, and see how it might be applied to your current life. What are the next steps you need to take to make the necessary changes? For instance, if the message you got from a past life is that family closeness is important, then what do you need to do in your busy schedule to make sure that you make time to be with your married daughter, or your teenage son, or your elderly father? If you live a life filled with stress, and in one or two or three of your past lives simplicity was the wisdom, then what steps do you need to take to allow yourself to become less cluttered in your mind body and spirit?

Give light, and the darkness will disappear of itself.
– Desiderius Erasmus

I've never been afraid to initiate new lines of thinking and new ways of being, or to set new standards. But sometimes I've felt like I was talking into the wind. People laughed at me because I talked about the protection of whales and dolphins in the 70s and 80s, and about the understanding that we are all connected, that the soul is transient, that we are all part of the universe.

And then I had a past life regression where I came into the life as a young man whose role was to amuse the ladies in a grand house in 18th century France. Their hair was high and elaborate and their dresses were huge and they sat around drinking tea. My role was to wander around singing for them and playing music on a three-stringed, big-bellied instrument. For a while I believed that they liked my music. Then I realized they weren't interested and weren't even listening. So I began to make up ribald, unflattering songs about them to amuse myself. The only time I got chastised was when I stopped. Then the mistress would become angry with me.

To look backward for a while is to refresh the eye, to restore it, and to render it more fit for its prime function of looking forward.
– Margaret Fairless Barber

When I got older, I was sent to the children's courtyard where I played for the children, who also didn't listen to me. But I didn't mind because I liked the children and loved to watch them play. I stayed there until I died and when I was asked what wisdom I could bring from that life, it was that "the music is still the music, even if nobody listens." And that message had such a profound impact on me, it made everything that I'd gone through and stood for, okay.

It confirmed for me that it doesn't matter what everybody else thinks, it's what I think and what I believe that matters. I'd always sort of known that, but now I KNEW it!

Trust Your Subconscious Mind

You have the choice. Your conscious mind is always active and aware when you are using hypnosis, and your subconscious mind will not allow you to go to a place you can't handle.

It's important to understand, however, that once you discover something that's been in your subconscious mind, once you know it, you can't "unknow" it. It will be with you always, and will have an impact on your life from now on.

If you are uncomfortable after your session, and feel you have issues you need to resolve or explore further, I suggest you find a therapist and discuss the issues that came up for you. There can be valid issues raised in a hypnosis or past life regression session that need to be discussed and evaluated. Remember why you decided to take this journey in the first place. Was it because you wanted to discover your purpose in this life? Was it to find out what has been holding you back from what you believe your purpose to be? Were you seeking answers to questions about affinities in your present life to places or historical periods?

You may not have found the answers to all your questions, and you may have raised more questions. Remember, this is a process of discovery. You are discovering yourself in all the experience, life lessons and wisdom gained from your past lives. All of it belongs to you. It's what makes you unique and truly yourself. We seek to understand ourselves and our place in the grand scheme of things because we are human, because we have minds that think and hearts that feel.

A man who carries a cat by the tail learns something he can learn in no other way
– Mark Twain

The real you, the immortal you, is the you that is present from body to body, from life to life. How exciting it is to meet yourself!
– Brian Weiss, *Through Time Into Healing*

CHAPTER 10

Case Histories And Healings

What you are is what you have been, and what you will be is what you do now.
– Gautama Buddha

The virtues we acquire, which develop slowly within us, are the invisible links that bind each one of our existences to the others – existences which the spirit alone remembers, for Matter has no memory for spiritual things.
– Honoré de Balzac

The more work I do around the soul journey, the more I am amazed by it. I feel humbled and privileged to work with clients during their journeys. Every good facilitator I've worked with, or trained, feels the same and comes to understand that they are only the facilitator. The client's soul is the miraculous part of the process.

Most people undertake the journey into a past life because they are curious. They may have heard or read about past life regression, or they have always felt a strong affinity for a particular place or time in history. Some have dreams that recur and that are very real to them.

Those who take the journey often come away with a better understanding about the connected-ness of life, and about who they are, and perhaps why they are that way. They need not be of a spiritual nature, and in fact, many are downright cynical at the beginning, but most inevitably find themselves opening up to new possibilities and a clearer sense of purpose.

A number of themes or ideas emerge from past life regression journeys. Whether the subjects are looking for healing, wisdom or some kind of understanding, the "life lessons" that they bring back with them from past lives are usually clear and pertinent to the lives they are living today.

Following are some of the people (their names have been changed) who have experienced past life regression at the clinic. The lessons and the wisdom are universal. Of necessity the cases have been abbreviated with only key points described.

Love

Client: Linda – Came into the clinic to discover the reason for a series of failed relationships

First Past Life Regression:
In her first past life, Linda said she was a female, wearing dainty black shoes, a black dress and black shawl. Her blonde hair was dirty and pinned up. She appeared to be in an older house with lots of stairs, a bar or pub, with lots of people, including cowboys, dancing, and being really loud. There were several girls wearing feathers and sequins. Her name was Jenny and she was 26. At night she slept in a single bed in a small room, above the bar, with a rotted wood floor and a light bulb hanging from the ceiling. There appeared to be a man she cared about, but at one point she

If you love all things, you will also attain the divine mystery that is in all things. For then your ability to perceive the truth will grow every day, and your mind will open itself to an all-embracing love.
– Fyodor Dostoyevsky

found herself in her room crying, with someone on the bed who had died of a heart attack.

She then saw herself outside the bar, where it was very quiet. The bar appeared to be closed for good and she was feeling very alone. She then found herself across from the pub, on a balcony, where she jumped and died.

Wisdom: *Linda believed the wisdom from that life was to be careful who you love; she hadn't been allowed to love and by choosing to go against the wisdom, loving had cost the person her life.*

Client: Annette – Wanted to let go of the pain of her childhood years.

First Past Life Regression:
Annette found herself a male, 20 years old, with dark skin, in a place where the houses were small and people were working, digging, and men carried baskets on their shoulders. A king appears in a procession and people begin to cheer. The king has a big dark beard and wears a small gold crown. His wife sits in a chair behind him.

He then finds himself working with the King, making plans for a school to be built, so he must be quite important. As an old man, he is a teacher, teaching a large number of children. When he is dying, people come to his home to pray over him and after his death he is carried through the town and people are singing.

Wisdom: Annette believed the lesson of the life was to be kind to people and help them. The wisdom was that love is the most important thing; that we can overcome anything with love.

Client: Sandra – Came in for personal exploration.

First Past Life Regression:
In her first past life, Sandra was a pilot dropping bombs in war. She said the pilot felt sadness, knowing he was killing innocent people. He hated war and the pain he was causing children. His reluctance to carry out his duty finally leads to him crashing his own plane.

Wisdom: Sandra believed the lesson of this life was to love the children.

Second Past Life Regression:
In her second past life, Sandra was a courtesan living a completely hedonistic life that included orgies. However, she died a peaceful death, surrounded by friends. The wisdom she gained from that life was to live for life, be bold and unafraid.

Wisdom: Despite the contrast between Sandra's two past lives, there was a love of life in both of them. One was forced to take life away and paid a high price for doing it, and the other grabbed life and celebrated it.

Client: Helen – To explore the cause of her depression, since childhood.

Past Lives:
Helen came to the clinic suffering from anxiety and depression, hoping past life regression would help her. She was regressed through three past lives, each of which had a lesson to teach.

In the first she had been in a loveless marriage. She took from that life the understanding that she needed to be emotionally stronger, to take hold of each moment and live now. In the second life, she and her husband were killed (scalped) on their wedding day. And in the third life, she was a woman whose face had been disfigured in a fire caused by her alcoholic father. Her brother looked after her for a while, but soon abandoned her. It was through the kindness of a religious man that she found a place to live and work in the service of a wealthy woman.

Wisdom: Through each of these lives ran the recurring theme that love mattered more than anything else, and that love could come in many forms and from many sources and she needed to be open to receive love in its many guises.

Family

Client: Elizabeth – Came in to explore why she focused on her family to the exclusion of everything and everyone else.

First Past Life Regression:
Elizabeth found herself outside, a female aged 12 with no shoes on. She was wearing an old dress with holes in it but surrounded by laughing children, two little boys and a girl. She saw her mother in a dark red dress and an apron, with her hair pinned up in a bun. The house they lived in was made of stone, and there were chickens in a shack attached to the house.

At some point some "scary guys" come into the house. Her mother is screaming and one of the men is yelling about something her father did. The men are hitting her mother and they grab her brother, taking him with them when they leave. She sees her mother covered in blood, her face swollen.

At some point her mother is ill, and Elizabeth and her sister are taking care of her. Eventually she dies and the two girls take their mother, wrapped in a cloth and put her in the water, where she begins to float away. She and her sister are alone and frightened, and Elizabeth goes into the water and swims away, saying she is "going to be with my mother." She sees her sister, standing alone and crying.

Wisdom: Elizabeth believes the wisdom from that life is that family is very important and we should enjoy it as part of the fabric of life. We are all family.

To put the world right in order, we must first put the nation in order; to put the nation in order, we must first put the family in order; to put the family in order, we must first cultivate our personal life; we must first set our hearts right.
– Confucius

Client: Betty – Came in to see if she could find the source of her loneliness.

First Past Life Regression:
Betty saw herself in Spain or Portugal as a middle-aged woman, near white sand and blue water. She was with her mother, on their last trip together. She was part of a large family with lots of children and cousins. They lived in the countryside, working hard and living off the land.

Wisdom: From that life Betty brought back the lesson that happiness comes from hard work, sharing and family.

Client: Bob – Was researching to discover more about himself.

First Past Life Regression:
Bob's first past life regression took him to a town or small village in the mountains. He was a male in his 30s wearing animal skins. He said he had lost his family and was very lonely. He seemed to be in Asia in the early 1500s.

A while later he is in a town of some sort, where there are women on the streets and monks with bowls, but they don't look at him. Someone brings him a bowl with rice, but he eats alone.

Eventually Bob found himself sick and in a bed in a place where there were a lot of other sick, dying and dead people around him. Someone takes care of him, bathes and feeds him, but there is no other treatment. He dies alone and broken, his hopes and dreams shattered.

Wisdom: Bob believed that life showed him the importance of family, that without family, there could be no home, no belonging.

The Power is Within Us

Client: Joyce – Came in out of curiosity.

First Past Life Regression:
Joyce was a barefoot male, about 25, in a jungle surrounded by exotic birds. He was hunting for food with a bow and arrow, hoping to get a bird or an animal for his family, that included his mother and sister.

At one point there is a big celebration with drums, chanting and dancing. Animals are being sacrificed in some sort of ritual. Joyce believed she was on an island, or possibly Australia or New Zealand.

When his mother becomes ill, a medicine man or healer blesses her, and as she passes, "an energy comes into my body," says Joyce.

Later the young man is playing with his son in the jungle, swinging on a long cord and jumping into the water. Caught unawares, he is grabbed by the neck and killed by a tiger, in front of his 12-year-old son.

Wisdom: Joyce brought back the wisdom of the medicine man, that the power to do whatever we want is within us.

Client: Charles – Needed to understand
his pain.

Not long ago a young man named Charles
came to the clinic suffering from depression
and anxiety. He was a financial analyst by
profession and the son of a banker. He had
always been drawn to the solitary life but had
rejected religion in his teens. Not long after,
he fell into a major depression, during which
he began to read everything he could find on
religion.

First Past Life Regression:
In his first past life regression, he was a monk
whose mission was to serve Christ with love
and compassion. When he returned to the
present, Charles was clearly disturbed by the
experience. He felt that he had avoided his
feelings in his current life and that he was not
upholding the values of dignity, tolerance,
justice and honor that his past life had taught
him.

Second Past Life Regression:
In his second past life regression Charles was
a cleric at a mosque in Mecca, around 1200.
He died defending the city against the
Crusaders when a sword was driven through
his heart. He believed the wisdom of that life
was that only through caring for and engaging
with others can we find happiness. He was
saddened, however, by the feeling that there
were limits to what one person could do to
protect their friends and family.

Third Past Life Regression:
Charles's third regression took him to the
Middle East where he had been a male slave

who was abused. This life's lesson, that when you lose faith in God you go adrift, had a profound impact on Charles.

Wisdom: Through the three past life regressions he underwent, Charles was able to put his present life into perspective and came to realize the source of his conflict with his family and their values. He made the decision to leave his career in business and go into teaching.

Joy in Life

Client: Adele – A student who wanted to know more.

First Past Life Regression:
Adele found herself in a very simple home at mealtime, eating salty oatmeal from a wooden bowl with two other children, a younger girl with blonde hair and a boy. Her father worked in the fields.

Suddenly they were leaving in a hurry, and Adele knew her mother was worried. It was dark and they were running away from a fire. The fields were on fire and people were gathering by a river trying to get across.

Later she found herself on a street in a town. She was about 20 years old and had a child with her and they were going somewhere. She was holding the child's hand and they were walking. The streets and buildings were made of stone. She was shopping and had coins to buy things with. It was her daughter's birthday and they were celebrating.

— 91 —

She arrives home after a long walk over a bridge, just outside of town. There are small cottages surrounded by rolling hills. Her husband, John, is tall, with a beard, and his clothes are dirty. He works very hard. They pray to God for work and food, but there are also happy times, with celebrations and festivals.

Then it is winter, cold with snow, but the fire keeps them warm. She is sewing, making clothes by candlelight. She's pregnant and feels heavy. At the birth, there are women around her, helping. The baby is a boy. He is fine but she is very tired, and dies soon after.

Wisdom: Adele believed the joy of that life was in her family, and although they were poor and didn't have much, they were happy.

Success is not fame or money or the power to bewitch. It is to have created something valuable from your own individuality and skill – a garden, an embroidery, a painting, a cake, a life.
– Charlotte Gray

Joy in Simplicity

Client: Ricardo – Wanted to understand himself more.

First Past Life Regression:
Ricardo's past life was as a woman in suede moccasins with black braids. She slept under the stars at night, away from some of the group. At one point there was a ceremony in which feather headdresses were worn, and there is much dancing as a form of release. She did not participate, but watched. The woman's role in the group was to take care of children, keep them out of danger and mend clothes.

The group or tribe she belongs to does not live in tipis. They are nomadic and move with the seasons, following the food.

Wisdom: The joy and wisdom in that life came from its simplicity, living with nature and raising children. It helped Ricardo understand in his present life, why he has always needed to travel and feels like an outsider.

Joy in Personal Happiness

Client: Bob – A corporate executive, wanted to explore his other self.

Third Past Life Regression:
In Bob's third past life regression, he was a 15-year-old male, living outside of the city near a rain forest. His home was very plain, made of mud-brick walls and he walked for transportation because there was no other way. He lived with his parents and a sister.

His father works with stone, as a carver, and creates monuments, but Bob wants to be a warrior and write poetry that tells of sacrifice and honor. Bob leaves the life when he is killed during a terrible battle.

Wisdom: Bob believes he got the most joy in that life from writing and art, but came to understand that there is no romance in violence. He was very young and embraced what was beautiful in life, but learned that the passions of the heart should be tempered by the mind, that no cause is so great that it supercedes personal happiness.

When one door of happiness closes, another opens; often we look so long at the closed door that we do not see the one that has been opened for us.
– Helen Keller

Responsibility

Client: Norah – Wanted to know why she feels so responsible for everyone.

Norah was a young woman who had never felt connected to her mother or her siblings, and was a tomboy during her childhood. She became a firefighter as an adult.

First Past Life Regression:
In her first past life regression, Norah was a Native Indian woman with a husband and children. When her husband died in battle, she was forced to live independently and ultimately died alone, but at peace. On returning to the present, she questioned whether she had dealt well with the grief in her life.

Second Past Life Regression:
In her second past life journey, Norah was a woman who joins a group in revolt against the king and is stabbed to death. She left the life wondering if she could have been more courageous.

Third Past Life Regression:
In her third past life regression, Norah is a male medicine maker in Africa who feels responsible when his patient dies. He is sent away and feels he has been treated unjustly. He is angry and bitter.

Wisdom: Norah carries a huge burden of responsibility in her present life. By choosing to be a firefighter, she is quite possibly attempting to assuage the feelings of guilt and inadequacy

she has brought forward from these past lives.
Being a firefighter may well be a way to healing
for Norah by balancing her soul.

Be True to Yourself

Client: Fiona – Came in for deeper self-understanding.

Fiona is a homeopathic doctor who always felt a strong affinity to Atlantis and all things Asian and oriental.

First Past Life Regression:
In her first past life, Fiona was a female in Switzerland in 1546, in love with a man who reminded her of her current husband. She marries him but he soon becomes irritating and demanding. She is disappointed – this is not what she had expected – and heartbroken. She leaves him and lives the next part of her life feeling lonely. She feels free only when he dies.

Wisdom: Fiona believes the lesson of that life is to learn to express her true feelings and to trust herself in her current life.

Second Past Life Regression:
In her second past life regression, Fiona was a young male philosophy teacher in Greece, in 560 BC. As he became older, he became quite well known, but he was sad because people would come to him for wisdom, but wouldn't follow his advice.

Wisdom: The wisdom that comes from that life, according to Fiona, is to follow your own path and know yourself.

Third Past Life Regression:
In her third past life regression, Fiona found herself in a temple in Atlantis. Her work was to instruct women to find their highest self. She believed she was a high priestess, someone with strong values, who was respected and who never wavered in her responsibility.

Wisdom: The wisdom of the life told her to believe in the power of women and their understanding.

Courage

Whatever you do, or dream you can, begin it; boldness has genius, power, and magic in it.
– Goethe

Client: Mark – An entrepreneur who wanted to understand himself more deeply.

First Past Life Regression:
In his first past life regression, Mark was a teenage male on a slave ship, unloading dead bodies. He was in England, probably around 1780. At some point he finds himself in port, a place with palm trees and people wearing sarongs. He meets a woman, has to leave, but eventually goes back to her, staying for a month. They have a daughter and other children, but his eldest son is killed in an accident.

Wisdom: Mark believed that the wisdom of the life was don't be afraid to give.

Second Past Life Regression:
In his second past life regression, Mark was a female in her 30s in the early 1900s, probably in America. She is a writer with no job, who writes stories she can't sell. She finally decides

to cut her hair, wear a suit and pretend to be a man. A publisher eventually buys one of her stories. She subsequently meets a man, who is her friend, and marries him.

Wisdom: The life lesson, according to Mark, is courage and tenacity: never give up.

Allergy Research and Past Life Connection

From September 2001 until November 2003 the Ontario Hypnosis Centre conducted a study to find out the root cause or the Initial Sensitizing Event (I.S.E.) of Allergy(s) to Animal(s). Twelve people from various walks of life participated in our study. The main allergens were cats, dogs and horses. We used Time Charting to find the root cause or I.S.E. of their allergy. Out of the 12 participants in our study, four individuals spontaneously went into a past life.

One participant experienced two past lives and one participant went into the womb as well as a past life. In each past life there was an emotional component directly related to an animal encounter. The only drawback to this amazing finding was that our study protocol did not allow for a complete past life regression. We did an abbreviated regression that included forgiveness, love and healing of that life. We then closed off the life, leaving behind all tendencies to allergic reactions to animals. Each participant was surprised to find that their allergy root cause had been from a past life experience.

Here is a brief description of each of the past lives.

Client: Participant A

A male about 38 years of age and in good health. He suffers from many different kinds of allergies, particularly to horses, cats and dogs.

Past Life
His spontaneous past life was as a cavalry soldier in the 1800s. "I can see a soldier riding a horse, a blue uniform with gold buttons, blonde hair, moustache. Like a civil war or Europe … He's riding into battle, he feels strong, a leader, holding a sword up, charging, charging towards hundreds of red soldiers coming the other way and toward him all lined up, on horses, and he has no fear."

Wisdom: The message from the past was "Fight. You know you're strong." Participant A said that most of his life he believed he couldn't do a number of things for fear of having a deadly allergic reaction. He had always felt weak and now he felt strong. His allergy symptoms have improved so much that he wants to get a dog.

Client: Participant B

A female around the age of 30 and in good health. Her allergies were to cats and dogs.

Past Life
In her first session Participant B spontaneously went back to a past life as a gray-colored cat in a cave. There were other cats in the cave, including one black cat that attacked and tore

open the gray cat. Because the experience did not involve language, the participant made only guttural sounds.

Wisdom: *The lesson was to forgive and to love the other cat. When participant B emerged from hypnosis her first words were, "I'm not a cat anymore." During the regression she had been aware of her lungs and a difficulty in breathing. This participant's asthmatic and allergy symptoms have improved slightly.*

During a third session Participant B journeyed back to the womb where she understood her mother had really wanted a dog but had a child instead.

Client: Participant C

A female around the age of 44 in excellent health. Her allergies were to cats, mice and rats. This participant journeyed to two past lives.

First Past Life Regression
The first was a spontaneous past life as a young male on his first hunt somewhere in Africa. He came face to face with a large cat like a cheetah with big red eyes and a very strong jaw. The cat was snarling and the young man ran away. He felt like a coward and was ashamed of himself. He felt he could have been braver and should have faced the cat. He lost standing in his village, shame came to his family and he was not allowed to marry the girl that he loved most.

Wisdom: *The lessons learned were about vulnerability and respect. Participant C's allergy symptoms have since decreased and she takes less medication since the discovery of a past life connection.*

Second Past Life Regression
In the next session Participant C went into a spontaneous past life as a young, male peasant sheepherder on the moors. The young sheepherder confronted a wolf attacking the sheep and killed the wolf by using his bow and arrow. "There is blood everywhere, it's all over my hands, it's all over me, I can't look at it ... I killed [the wolf] and I'm so disgusted with [the blood]. I can't wash it off, it feels horrible." For religious reasons participant C could not do the forgiveness part of Regression. At a follow-up Regression one month later Participant C said he takes 50% less medication than before starting the Allergy(s) to Animal(s) Study.

Client: Participant D

A female around the age of 37. She was in good health with no prolonged illness. Her allergies are to cats, dogs and horses.

First Past Life Regression
In the first session participant D did not believe she had been hypnotized.

Second Past Life Regression
In the second session Participant D spontaneously went into a past life in the 1700s or 1800s in France as a young male page. He was wearing "pointy shoes, floppy shoes with

a bell on the end, white leotards, and a turquoise page outfit with gold beads and a turquoise and gold turban on his head." The next significant event in his life was when he was shipwrecked on an island with a cat. They both began to go mad and the cat attacked him. "The cat is on my back, and it's digging its nails into my back ... I grabbed the cat and I'm shaking if off and it's clawing back at me ... I have a lot of cuts on my hands and my legs. I think it wants to eat me." Participant D then began to laugh. "I think I showed that cat ... I'm crying now. I'm angry at that cat and it's his fault. If he hadn't bitten me, I wouldn't have been angry at it. Now I'm very lonely."

Wisdom: The lesson learned was "I shouldn't have eaten my friend." We did forgiveness work, love and healing of the past life, leaving behind the allergy to cats. When participant D emerged from hypnosis she still did not believe that she had gone into a past life or was even hypnotized. She explained she has a very creative imagination and that's all it was. At the time of this printing participant D's follow-up has not been completed to find out what effect the past life has had on her allergic reaction to cats.

With this new information from the data collected from these four Allergy(s) to Animal(s) participants' past lives, I feel further studies into Allergy(s) to Animal(s) are warranted with a more in-depth and complete look into the possibility that a past life may play a role in allergies to animal(s) symptoms. Future studies into a past life connection to allergies to animal(s) may yield healing and closure to those suffering from allergies in their present lives brought on by an Initial Sensitizing Event from the past.

Unless you walk out into the unknown, the odds of making a profound difference in your life are pretty low.
– Tom Peters

CHAPTER 11

Where Can You Go From Here?

The purpose of life is to discover your gift.
The meaning of life is giving your gift away.
– David Viscott, psychiatrist & writer

YOU WILL FIND THAT THE MORE you explore your soul journeys, the more profound and insightful is the wisdom you gain. Rather than focus on who you were and where you were, consider using your regressions to add depth, understanding and wisdom to your current life.

Chart each life, using the Memories Chart in the Addenda of this book, and see what your patterns are. If they are negative or harmful in any way to you in this lifetime, plan how to end the patterns ... so that you won't repeat them!

Remember this is a planet of free will, which means we have total choice in how we conduct ourselves.

Know also, that we carry forward beneficial patterns and traits, so consider how you might use all of those to maximum advantage in your current life. As you look back and see yourself – a different sex, a different color, a different shape, different economic and social status – it helps to understand that we are all the same.

We are all good, all bad, all smart and all stupid. We can be kind, evil, straightforward and manipulative. We contain every type of emotion and behavior ... but it's what we do with who we are, the choices we make, that make us the person we are in this lifetime, on this planet.

The Here and Now ... and Hereafter

This life – the here and now – is the most important time. Do what you can every day to celebrate this lifetime, to live each moment fully and with respect. If you decide to journey back, make sure the here and now is the best it can be ... for now.

Always keep the following things in mind –

- Have you left things with those you love the way you want to leave them?

- Are the last things you said what you want remembered about you?

- Have you left anything undone ... or unsaid?

- How important is that issue that irritates you?

- What is your legacy ... how will you be remembered?

- What will you be honored and loved for?

When we die and go to heaven, our Maker is not going to say, why didn't you discover the cure for such and such? The only thing we're going to be asked at that precious moment is why didn't you become you?
– Elie Wiesel

My wish is that you use your journeys to encourage your mental, physical and emotional health and well-being, and that you find the wisdom a gateway into joy and curiosity for this lifetime as you are living it now.

Live as if you would die tomorrow,
learn as if you would live forever.

– Mahatma Gandhi

CHARTING YOUR MEMORIES

LIFE 1	
DETAILS	
LESSONS LEARNED	
ACTIONS FOR THIS LIFE	

CHARTING YOUR MEMORIES

LIFE 2	
DETAILS	
LESSONS LEARNED	
ACTIONS FOR THIS LIFE	

CODE OF CONDUCT FOR ETHICAL CLIENT-CENTERED PAST LIFE RESEARCH AND REGRESSION JOURNEYS

Ethical Past Life Regression Journeys are the experience of the client and in no way reflect the thoughts, feelings or channelings of the facilitator or practitioner.

1. The client experiences the journey in a kind, safe and trusting environment.
2. Soul Permission is asked before embarking on the journey.
3. Protection and help is asked before embarking on the journey.
4. Upon completion of the life, forgiveness, compassion and love are given to the person in that lifetime.
5. Upon completion of the life, forgiveness, compassion and love are given to those who shared that life with the client.
6. Joy and wisdom from that life are explored and brought forward into the current day.
7. The life is closed off leaving all pain and discomfort behind the veil.
8. The client is returned in fullness to the current time and place and encouraged to document and bring wisdom and learning into their current lifetime.

As a fully trained client-centered past life regression facilitator, I promise and commit to the above code of ethics and practice.

Name _____ Date _____

Issued by The Ontario Hypnosis Centre Clinic and School, Toronto, Ontario, Canada

REFERENCES

CHAPTER ONE
Barbara Findeisen quote is from Winafred Blake Lucas, *Regression Therapy,*
  Vol.I, page 23
Henry Bolduc, *Life Patterns*, page 9

CHAPTER TWO
Study by Winafred Lucas, Ph.D., quoted from International Board of
  Regression Therapies (IBRT) Web site
Carl Rogers quote from Sylvia Cranston, *Reincarnation*, page 45
Study by Helen Wambach, Ph.D., quoted from IBRT Web site
Henry Bolduc, *The Journey Within*, page 109

CHAPTER THREE
Dr. Ian Stevenson quote from Jeffrey Iverson, *In Search of the Dead*
Carol Bowman quote from *Children's Past Lives*
Dr. Brian Weiss, *Through Time Into Healing*, page 158
Roger Woolger, PhD, quote from *Other Lives, Other Selves,* found on
  Healpastlives Web site
The Dhammapada. Verses 419, 423

CHAPTER FOUR
Dr. Bruce Goldberg quote from *Past Lives, Future Lives*
Michael Gabriel quote from *Remembering Your Life Before Birth*
Dr. Brian Weiss, *Through Time Into Healing*, page 55

CHAPTER FIVE
Rudolf Steiner quote from Joel L. Whitton, *Life Between Life*, p. 25
Prof. Hans J. Eysenck quote from Jeffrey Iverson, *In Search of the Dead,*
  page 35
Dr. Ian Stevenson quote from Jeffrey Iverson, *In Search of the Dead*, page xi

CHAPTER SIX
Sylvia Browne, *Past Lives, Future Healing*, page 21
William J. Baldwin, *Spirit Releasement Therapy*, page 7
Carl Rogers quote from "Some New Directions: A Personal View," in
  Thomas Hanna, *Explorers of Humankind*
Ted Andrews, *How to Uncover Your Past Lives*, pages 117-118

CHAPTER SEVEN
Henry Bolduc, *Life Patterns*, page 59
Ted Andrews, *How to Uncover Your Past Lives*, page 11
Henry Bolduc, *Life Patterns*, page 60
Henry Bolduc, *The Journey Within*, page 101

CHAPTER EIGHT
Henri Bolduc, *The Journey Within*, pages 298-99

CHAPTER NINE
Deepak Chopra, *How to Know God*, pages 239-241
Brian Weiss, *Through Time Into* Healing, p.184
Brian Weiss, *Through Time Into Healing*, p. 185

BIBLIOGRAPHY

Andrews, Ted. *How To Uncover Your Past Lives*. St. Paul, MN: Llewellyn Publications, 1997

Baldwin, William J. and Edith Fiore. *Spirit Releasement Therapy: A Technique Manual*. Headline Books, 1992

Bolduc, Henry Leo. *The Journey Within: Past-Life Regression and Channeling*. Independence, VA: Adventures Into Time Publishers, 1988

——————. *Life Patterns: Soul Lessons & Forgiveness*. Independence, VA: Adventures Into Time Publishers, 1994

Bowman, Carol. *Children's Past Lives: How Past Life Memories Affect Your Child*. NY: Bantam Books, 1997

Brennan, J.H. *The Reincarnation Workbook: A Complete Course in Recalling Past Lives*. Wellingborough, GB: The Aquarian Press, 1989

Browne, Sylvia. *Life on the Other Side: A Psychic's Tour of the Afterlife*. NY: Signet, 2000

——————. *The Other Side and Back: A Psychic's Guide to Our World and Beyond*. NY: Signet, 2000

——————. *Past Lives, Future Healing: A Psychic Reveals the Secrets to Good Health and Good Relationships*. NY: Dutton, 2001

Chopra, Deepak. *How To Know God: The Soul's Journey into the Mystery of Mysteries*. NY: Harmony Books, 2000

Cranston, Sylvia and Carey Williams. *Reincarnation: A New Horizon in Science, Religion, and Society*. NY: Julian Press, 1984

Evans-Wentz, W.Y., trans. *The Tibetan Book of the Dead*

Fiore, Edith, *You Have Been Here Before: A Psychologist Looks at Past Lives*. NY: Ballantine Books, 1986

Gabriel, Michael and Marie Gabriel. *Remembering Your Life Before Birth: How Your Womb Memories Shaped Your Life & How to Heal Them*. Aslan Publishing, 1995

Gershom, Rabbi Yonassan. *Beyond the Ashes: Cases of Reincarnation from the Holocaust*. A.R.E. Press, 1992

Goldberg, Dr. Bruce. *Past Lives, Future Lives*. NY: Ballantine Books, 1988

Hanna Thomas. *Explorers of Humankind*. San Francisco: Harper & Row, 1979

Iverson, Jeffrey. *In Search of the Dead: A Scientific Investigation of Evidence for Life after Death*. London: Penguin Group and BBC Enterprises, 1992

Lucas, Winafred Blake, PH.D. *Regression Therapy: A Handbook for Professionals*, Vols. I and II. Crest Park, CA: Deep Forest Press, 1996

Shroder, Thomas. *Old Souls: Compelling Evidence from Children Who Remember Past Lives*. NY: Simon & Schuster, 2001

Stearn, Jess. *Edgar Cayce: The Sleeping Prophet*. NY: Bantam Books, 1967

Steiger, Brad. *You Will Live Again: Dramatic Case Histories of Reincarnation*. Blue Dolphin Publishing, 1996

Stevenson, Dr. Ian. *Children Who Remember Previous Lives: A Question of Reincarnation*. McFarland & Co., 2000

TenDam, Hans. *Exploring Reincarnation: The Classic Guide to the Evidence for Past-Life Experiences*. Arkana, 1990

Weiss, Dr. Brian. *Many Lives, Many Masters*. NY: Fireside, 1988

————. *Through Time into Healing: Discovering the Power of Regression Therapy to Erase Trauma and Transform Mind, Body, and Relationships*. NY: Fireside, 1993

Whitton, Joel L., M.D., PH.D., and Joe Fisher. *Life Between Life: Scientific Explorations into the Void Separating One Incarnation from the Next*. NY: Warner Books, 1986

Woolger, Roger J. *Other Lives, Other Selves: A Jungian Psychotherapist Discovers Past Lives*. NY: Bantam, 1988

INDEX

G
Gabriel, Michael, 37
Gandhi, Mahatma, 26, 104
Goethe, 96
Goldberg, Bruce, 37
Grandma Moses, 11
Gray, Charlotte, 92

H
healing, 17, 23, 33, 37-38
Herder, J.G., 46
Hinduism, 25-26
homeostasis, karmic, 4-5
hypnosis, 11-12, 35, 48-49,
    53-54
    see also self-hypnosis

I
imagination, 12-13
interlife *see* Bardo
invocation, 66
Ivanova, Varvara, 25

J
Janeway, Kathryn, 51
Jung, Carl, 23-24, 55

K
Karma, 25-26, 28
Keller, Helen, 93

L
Lammers, Arthur, 19
Lao Tse, 17
lessons, 32
    see also wisdom
life between lives, 42, 43-44
Lincoln, Abraham, 12
London, Jack, 29
Lucas, Winafred B., 4, 11, 21-22

M
meditation, 48, 53
memory, 49
mind, conscious and
    subconscious, 11

N
Nehru, Jawaharlal, 26
Nietzsche, Friedrich, 94
Nirvana, 27, 28

P
pain, 41
past life journey, 3-4
    and handling fear, 57-58
    issues arising from, 77, 81
    and life between lives, 42,
    43-44
    questions to ask, 62
    scripts, 66-76
past life regression, 34, 36
    and allergy research, 97-101
    benefits of, 17, 60
    and children, 21, 45-47
    process, 63-65
    questions about, 40-42
    and science, 45-46
    and the superconscious, 51
    see also reincarnation; soul
    journey
past lives, 34-36
    and choosing, 32
    clues to, 29-31
    see also case histories
patterns, 77
Patton, George S., 30
permission, 9
Peters, Tom, 101
phobias, 38
physics, 7, 8
proof, 15-16
protection, 9
Proust, Marcel, 15, 61

WEB SITES

ARE
Association for Research & Enlightenment
The Edgar Cayce Foundation
www.are-cayce.com

Childen's Past Lives Research Center
www.childpastlives.org

IARRT
International Association for
Regression Research & Therapies Inc.
www.iarrt.org

IBRT
International Board for Regression Therapies
www.ibrt.org

SEND US YOUR STORIES!

Do you have an interesting Past Life Regression Story that affected you dramatically and could fit into one of these categories?

- A physical health change
- A major life change
- How your journey helped you beat the odds
- or change your Karma
- or led you to your current life partner
- or introduced you to your soul mate

If your story is appropriate for one of our future books and we would like to include it, we'll give you full name credit – if you wish. If your story fits into our book outline we will contact you to receive your approval and find out more! It could be fun!

Send your stories to:

georgina_cannon@returntopastlife.com
or
Dr. Georgina Cannon,
Director, Ontario Hypnosis Centre,
94 Cumberland Street, #310,
Toronto. Ont. M5R 1A3
Canada

Also … Now that you've read this book, maybe you'd like to see more books like this. Take a few minutes and check out our Web site at:

www.ont-hypnosis-centre.com

and let me know if there's something there you would like to learn more about – in the same easy-to-read and absorbing style as this book. I'm currently working on my next two books and am always interested in hearing from readers about what interests them.

If you send me your thoughts about another book, I promise to respond personally to you. You can write to me about your new book idea at georgina_cannon@returntopastlife.com

Learn Hypnosis With Our Hypnosis Training Courses

and become a Past Life Regression Facilitator. The first step on your path is to

Take our Hypnosis Training Course and become a certified NGH Hypnotist!

Course Accredited by the largest international body of hypnotherapists, the National Guild of Hypnotists

Graduates may apply for membership to the **International Hypnotherapy Federation and The International Medical and Dental Hypnotherapy Association**

You will be able to use the powerful tool of clinical hypnosis to enable yourself, or your clients in smoking cessation, weight control, stress management, self esteem, pain management and goal setting techniques.

Upon graduation you'll also be qualified to run group hypnosis sessions for smoking cessation, weight loss, relaxation and goal setting.

Levels One and Two of this program are given at one time, so that you may practice immediately upon graduation. The program features small groups, lively and interactive learning, combined with a warm, helpful environment for your success.

- This pragmatic intensive curriculum is designed to allow the practitioner to practice the classical approach to hypnosis.

- You will learn the appropriate and approved applications for hypnosis, client assessment, trance techniques and client self-hypnosis techniques.

- Course includes two 100-page workbooks for ongoing learning, all video and audio tapes, induction and testing sheets, chevreuils pendulum and other materials for successful client work.

- On graduation you will receive a diploma and be accredited by the National Guild of Hypnotists

- Graduates have an automatic one-year membership in the National Guild of Hypnotists, which entitles you to:
  - Referrals through computer listings
  - Hypno-Gram quarterly newsletter
  - Journal of Hypnotism quarterly magazine
  - Video rental library for members
  - Annual Conference
  - Book, tape, and video discounts
  - Hotel/motel and auto rental discounts in the U.S.
  - Continuing education programs.

Contact: www.ont-hypnosis-centre.com for more information.

The Past Life Regression Facilitator Course
is based on the work of Henry Bolduc,
Dr Milton Erickson and Edgar Cayce

Because clients who are hypnotized sometimes "slip into" past or former lives when working to change something in their current life, the professional hypnotherapist needs to understand how to work in this field in an effective, healing and ethical way. This is a soul journey process which includes forgiveness, healing and wisdom. We also cover life between lives and the journey and decisions made before birth, Karma and choice.

- A three-day, intense, pragmatic, interactive and profound training program
- Past Lives, between lives, the decision and journey to this life
- Bringing forward the wisdom and understanding the relationships around the current life
- Researching for mental, physical or emotional pain
- Unique intuition expansion sessions
- Group and one-on-one practice sessions

A spiritual and profound three days that will make a difference to your life!

For further information contact us at www.ont-hypnosis-centre.com.

Order Your FREE
Past Life Regression CD

If you can't find your way to a Past Life Regression Facilitator, you might want to experience the journey through the power of your CD player!

As our gift to you, we will send you the CD "Past Life Memories" – absolutely free. Retail Price is usually $22.50. Because we want you to understand our passion and commitment to this process, all we ask is that you pay $5.00 for shipping and handling.

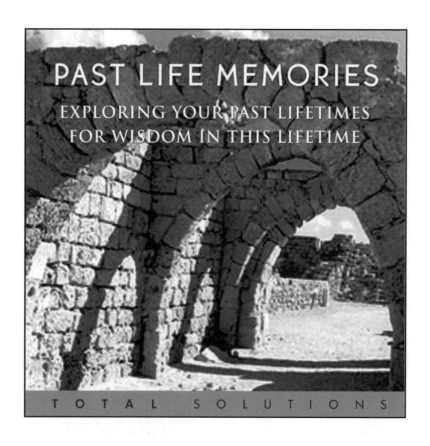

PAST LIFE MEMORIES
EXPLORING YOUR PAST LIFETIMES
FOR WISDOM IN THIS LIFETIME

TOTAL SOLUTIONS

CD LIST

ALL CD'S ARE $22.50 PLUS APPLICABLE TAXES AND SHIPPING.
FOR BULK ORDERS, PLEASE CONTACT:
info@ont-hypnosis-centre.com

1. **HEALING THE BODY** — This healing CD program will enable you to prepare your body for surgery or heal chronic or acute conditions by communicating with your body at the very deepest, cellular level.

2. **PAST LIFE MEMORIES** — Explore past lifetimes, safely and ethically, with this self-hypnosis CD.

3. **MOVE FORWARD WITH CONFIDENCE FOR WOMEN** — Find the confidence and creativity to move forward in your life, and make changes NOW.

4. **HYPERTENSION RELEASE** — A self-hypnosis journey to lifelong health and balance, enabling the reduction of hypertension once and for all.

5. **STOP SNORING** — Sleep deeply and quietly every night with this self-hypnosis program.

6. **LETTING GO OF STRESS** — An empowering, decompressing self-hypnosis program for anyone who needs to relax and allow the world to be a stress-free place.

7. **CREATING ABUNDANCE** — Create success, joy and love in your life. Let self-hypnosis help you to manifest the abundance you seek.

8. **STOP SMOKING FOR LIFE** — Take back control and be smoke-free for life with this self-hypnosis program.

9. **JOURNEY TO THE AKASHIC RECORDS** — Using the power of hypnosis, you can enjoy a spiritual soul journey that will enable you to find your soul purpose, your soul name, and maybe even your soul mate.

10. **IMPROVE YOUR SEXUAL PERFORMANCE** — Dream, explore and rediscover the possibilities of your own sensuality and sexuality.

11. **STARTING OVER** — This is an empowering self-hypnosis program that uses two voices for maximum success to access the left and right sides of your brain — both the creative and pragmatic parts — to enable you to move forward in life.

12. **RELAX AND REJUVENATE** — A renewal of self to refresh and relax your energy. Using the power of hypnosis, learn to bring harmony and balance back into your life.

13. **SLEEP ANYWHERE, ANYTIME** — This gentle self-hypnosis CD teaches you how to ease into sleep wherever and whenever you wish. Awake in the morning feeling refreshed and ready for your day.

14. **CHAKRA BALANCING** — A gentle hypnotic journey to balance and rejuvenate mind, body and spirit. Harmonize and explore your Chakras, their meaning and energies.

15. **ENLIGHTEN UP FOR LASTING WEIGHT LOSS** —This is a step-by-step weight loss program that is designed to increase your self-esteem, build your inner strength, and bring focus to your inner goals and life.

About the Author

DR. GEORGINA CANNON, a certified master clinical hypnotherapist, is an international award-winning teacher, lecturer and director of a hypnosis clinic and school in Toronto, Canada. In the seven years since its founding, Dr. Cannon has initiated the ethical protocols and procedures for regression now followed by her students and many others in the regression field.

Often called upon by radio, television and print media, Dr. Cannon is currently involved in a major network television series on past life regression, working on camera with over 30 volunteers. Dr. Cannon also meets regularly with medical and wellness professionals to enhance their knowledge and awareness of hypnosis and the dynamic healing potential of soul, or past life journeys.

Dr. Cannon is on the advisory board of the National Guild of Hypnotists